The Complete
Flower Arranging Book

The Complete Flower Arranging Book

SUSAN CONDER · SUE PHILLIPS · PAMELA WESTLAND

NORTH LIGHT BOOKS

$\mathscr{A}$CKNOWLEDGEMENTS

The Publishers wish to thank the following photographers and organisations
for their kind permission to reproduce their photographs and artwork:

C. Arber: 77; J Bouchier: 41, 42, 43; Camera Press: 44, 174; C. Crofton: 73, 74, 75;
EWA: 139; D. Garcia; 47, 48, 49, 105, 125, 128, 129, 157, 159, 160, 161; N. Hargreaves: 19, 29, 59, 64,
76, 77(b), 85, 150; Insight/Linda Burgess: 151; R. McMahon: 12, 13, 21, 22, 23, 24, 25,
26, 27, 45, 51, 52, 53, 55, 56, 57, 69, 70, 71, 82, 83, 108, 109, 111, 112, 113, 122, 123, 126, 127, 135,
136, 137, 138, 140, 141, 142, 143, 145, 146, 147, 163, 164, 165, 166, 167, 175, 177, 178,
179, 188, 189; Moben Kitchens/Jackie Chamley: 172; Photos Horticultural: 30; M. Plomer; 79, 80, 81;
M. Smallcombe: 33, 34, 35, 37, 38, 39, 61, 62, 63, 65, 66, 67, 87, 88, 89, 91, 92, 93, 95,
96, 97, 117, 118, 119, 131, 132, 133, 149, 152, 153, 154, 155, 169, 170, 171, 183, 184, 185, 187;
J. Suett: 121; R. Weller: 99, 100, 101, 103; Zefa: 18; Artwork: W. Giles: 17, 94, 102, 445,
115, 161; M. Leeder: 20; Gillie Newman: 8, 9, 14, 15; J. Pickering: 36, 68, 78, 186; S. Pond 32, 40, 46,
72, 120, 130, 134, 156, 161, 182 Octopus Publishing Group Limited/ Steve Bicknell: 181
Constance Spry Foundation/Martin Brigdale: 6, 180A; James Jackson: 2; Steve Lyne: 107;
Duncan McNicol: 173; Jerry Harpur: 46, 50; Jon Harris: 31; Herbie Smitz: 180B; George Wright: 54.

The Publishers are grateful for the help of the following: Pamela Westland,
Gail Armitage, Edel Brosnan, Anabel Carter, Carole Clements, Laura Lee,

Edited by Sophy Roberts Designed by Pauline Bayne
Production: Michele Thomas
Index: Myra Clark

This compilation first published in 1992 by Octopus Illustrated Publishing,
a division of Reed International Books Limited, Michelin House, 81 Fulham Road, London SW3 6RB

First published in the United States by North Light Books,
F&W Publications, Inc., 1507 Dana Avenue, Cincinnati, Ohio 45207
1-800-289-0963

The material in this book was originally published in 1988 by Orbis Publishing Limited.

ISBN 0891 34454 3

Produced by Mandarin Offset
Printed and bound in Hong Kong

Contents

Introduction

Flower arranging is an art that enhances our surroundings, adding a beautiful and personal touch to each room in the home. Floral displays can transform a dull hallway or brighten a dark corner, and they can bring an important finishing touch to your decoration scheme. Creating floral arrangements is an enjoyable and rewarding pastime that is based more on techniques than on artistic talent. It is a pleasurable craft everyone can learn.

The Complete Flower Arranging Course starts at the beginning, with the basic tools and equipment needed, including florist's foam, prongs, tape and containers. It explains how to select or cut flowers for arranging and how to condition them so they last well. Essential design principles of proportion, balance, contrast and harmony, are explained and illustrated with step-by-step arrangements.

The book explores colour and the ways it can be used to create various effects, using monochromatic themes, subtle harmonious shades from the same family or vivid contrasting colours. The classic shapes for arrangements are also shown, all with step-by-step photographs to guide you. Creative comparisons offer novel ideas for different ways to arrange the same flowers. You will see how with a bunch of tulips you can create an elegant fan-shaped arrangement, a striking Oriental effect or a massed block like you might find in a garden.

With an understanding of basic skills and principles, the possibilities for design are expanded. Innovative creations, such as an all-foliage display or combining herbs and vegetables with floral material, are exciting to assemble and give impressive results. Clear step-by-step photographs make even a tower of fruit and flowers easy to accomplish.

Along with acquiring expertise with fresh flowers. The Complete Flower Arranging Course offers techniques and inspiration for dried floral material. You will learn the methods for drying and preserving flowers and seedheads, providing the ingredients for long-lasting displays of all shapes and sizes. Using these materials, you can produce appealing arrangements, from a charming country basket display to a sophisticated dried flower tree, all fully illustrated to ensure successful results.

The creative use of containers provides another arena for building on your floral knowledge. Try some of the intriguing multiple vase groupings or create a Victorian look with miniature arrangements. Cover a plain box with moss to set off a naturalistic dried flower display or explore adventurous containers such as a tapestry bag.

Special occasions give you ample opportunity for more elaborate creations. You can set the mood with flowers – a lacy light-hearted basket display for a casual gathering or a more ornate formal arrangement in a silver punchbowl for a christening reception. Candleholders lend themselves to an array of treatments. You will learn how to use small containers for arrangements that fit right into the candelabra for a stunning effect, with the glow of the candlelight adding to the charm of the flowers.

The craft of flower arranging gives pleasure both to the creator of the displays and to all those who see them whether young or old, male or female.

The best way to learn and gradually develop your own style is by making many different kinds of arrangement, and the step-by-step illustrations and comprehensive information in this book will give you all the help and inspiration you need. Flower arranging is a relaxing and rewarding pastime which adds immeasurably to daily life, so get started and revel in the joy of flowers.

CHAPTER ONE

GETTING STARTED

You can create lovely flower displays with scissors alone, but having a few basic tools makes preparing and arranging flowers easier. Your local florist can supply many items, or order them for you from a specialist. Garden centres, hardware and department stores are other sources. If you join a local flower arranging club, you can often bulk-buy items at reduced rates. Always buy the best you can afford.

CUTTING TOOLS

Sharp kitchen scissors will do for soft stems, but florist's scissors with serrated blades are better, and can cut wire and tough stems. Use double-bladed secateurs to cut woody stems and garden flowers and foliage; single-blade types can crush stems. If you don't have florist's scissors, use wire cutters (not secateurs!) to cut florists' and chicken wire. Use a sharp kitchen or pocket knife to cut florist's foam.

SUPPORTS

Florist's, or floral, foam is a light-weight, synthetic support, fixed in a container or on a base, to hold stiff stems at the angle inserted. Floral foam for fresh displays is soaked in water before use. Rectangular foam blocks are cheapest, and can be cut to fit, but foam spheres, cones and cylinders are also sold. Prongs, spikes or 'frogs', are small, plastic, spiked discs fixed onto florist's mastic in the container base, for impaling the foam support. The mastic is like thin, green plasticine strips; household blue mastic can also be used. Pinholders,

or needle-points, are heavy metal bases with tightly packed, small, upright pins, onto which stems are impaled. They feature in Oriental flower displays, and come in many sizes and shapes. Crumpled chicken wire, or wire-mesh netting, is used to support large, heavy stems; it can also be wrapped round florist's foam, to reinforce it.

WIRING EQUIPMENT

Wiring flowers is a specialist skill, used in wedding bouquets and other formal displays. Cut lengths of wire, or stub wire, and fine reel wire, sold on spools, can also be used to make false stems, and wire clusters of stems together. Both come in a range of gauges and lengths. Adhesive, or florist's tape, is sticky on one side. Commonly green, it is used to conceal wired stems, and to secure foam to a container.

EXTRAS

Liquid or crystal cut-flower food added to vase water prolongs cut-flower life, and keeps water clean. A bucket is useful for conditioning flowers, and bleach and a nail brush, for cleaning containers.

THE BASIC ESSENTIALS

The following pieces of equipment are those which will be of most use to you when starting out as a budding flower arranger.

A sharp, general purpose **knife** or **floristry scissors** (special scissors with a serrated edge) are a must for cutting flower and foliage stems.

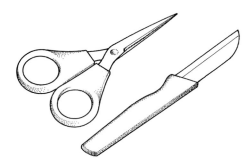

Florist's foam or floral foam. This is a lightweight synthetic spongy material that can be cut to fit any shape of container. It's useful for holding flowers with fairly stiff stems (the soft sappy stems of flowers like daffodils can't be pushed into florist's foam). It comes in two colours: green and brown. The brown is for dried arrangements and the green foam (which must be soaked in water before use) is for fresh flowers. Both types are available from florist's in a variety of shapes and sizes – in brick shapes for low arrangements, cylinder shapes for high ones, and cones and spherical shapes for more fancy designs.

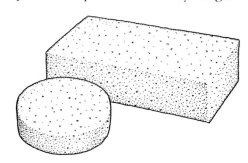

Wire cutters should be used when items that are too tough for your floristy scissors to cope with need cutting. They are exactly the right implements to use when snipping stiff stub wires and chicken wire.

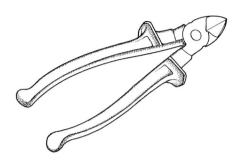

Use **secateurs** for cutting heavy stems and foliage and flowers from the garden. Do not use them for cutting wires or you will blunt them very quickly.

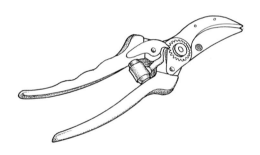

Prongs, spikes or 'frogs', as they are sometimes called, can also be bought at any florist. The most commonly used type of prong is a small plastic disc with four spikes. It is fixed to the bottom of a vase with a blob of adhesive clay and is used to hold block's of florist's foam in place.

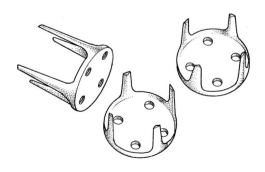

Chicken wire is a fine wire mesh that can be used as a stem support in some arrangements. Just 'scrunch' it up into a loose ball to fit a particular vase or container. Chicken wire is available from most hardware stores.

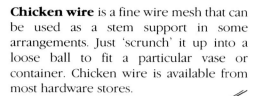

Adhesive tape or florist's tape (just like sticky tape) is sticky on one side and used to secure foam to a container.

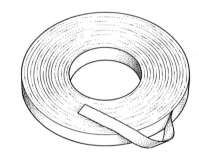

Pinholders are holding aids for large arrangements, and for top-heavy flowers with thick woody stems like chrysanthemums. A pinholder is simply a round, flat heavy weight with lots of pins sticking up from the base. A medium-sized holder with a diameter of about 6.5cm (2.5 in) is most useful to start with. Once you get more advanced, you will find florists stock pinholders in a variety of shapes and sizes.

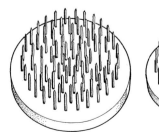

Stub wires are used in both fresh and dried arrangements for making false stems, wiring clusters of stems together, or for more intricate work where flowers need to be wired into a permanent shape such as in wedding bouquets. Stub wires are available in a wide range of lengths and gauges.

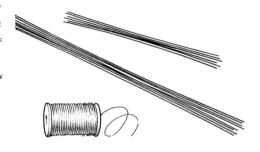

Cut-flower feed from florists and many stores is available in liquid or crystal form and can be added to vase water to prolong the life of flowers.

Adhesive clay or flower arranger's fixative is rather like plasticine, but sold in thin strips on a roll – again from the florist – and sticks well to dry, non-porous and shiny surfaces.

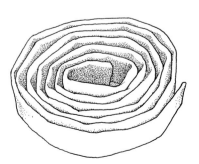

Techniques

There are a few basic techniques for securing flowers and foliage that you should master to be sure of a professional finish in your flower arrangements – whether they are dried or fresh. As long as you keep in mind the straight-forward steps and advice outlined on the following pages, you should be able to tackle any of the arrangements featured throughout the book, as well as feeling confident of making up designs of your own.

HOLDING FLOWERS IN PLACE

Some of the most fashionable flower arranging styles nowadays don't use any holding aids at all; instead flower stems are allowed to bend naturally. But it's generally easier to get flowers looking their best in an arrangement by using florist's foam, chicken wire or a pinholder to support the stems. Oriental-style displays often use forked twigs across the neck of the containers to hold stems in place. Occasionally, sticky-tape is used as a holding device.

THE MOST POPULAR SUPPORT

Floral foam is the commonest item used by arrangers to hold flower stems in place. Widely available from florist shops and garden centres, foam is made from synthetic substances and is sold in blocks or pre-formed shapes but can be cut to fit different-shaped containers. The sort of foam used for fresh flowers is usually green, general-purpose foam. This is suitable for most flowers with fairly stiff stems, such as carnations.

USING A PINHOLDER

To use a pinholder, just stick it to the bottom of a vase with a blob of adhesive clay and press flower stems gently down, either between the spikes or down onto them, depending on the thickness of the stems, and spacing between the spikes.

Like vases, pinholders need to be washed well in a mixture of warm water and bleach and rinsed in clean water before you store them away for future use.

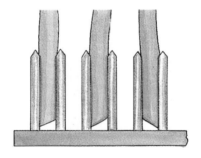

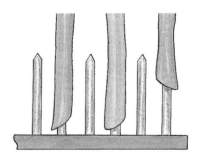

USING CHICKEN WIRE

Chicken wire is used less frequently than florist's foam these days in arrangements. It can be difficult to work with and will not hold flower stems as precisely as foam. However, for a really large arrangement made up of heavy materials such as branches, a loose ball of fine wire mesh, 2.5-5cm (1-2 ins) in diameter, crumpled up to fill a wide-necked vase or container until it grips the inside surfaces, still makes the best 'base'.

USING FLORIST'S FOAM

only absorb water on the outside and the middle will be left completely dry. When the foam bobs up again level with the surface of the water and has turned dark green, it will have absorbed all the water it needs. Soaking the foam takes no more than a minute or two, depending on size, then it's ready to be used.

and it will be held perfectly firmly. If the container you want to use in your arrangement is not waterproof, then fix your foam to a small concealable waterproof tray and tape securely with a length of florist's adhesive tape to the container.

1 The block of foam that you buy will usually be far too large or the wrong shape to fit into your chosen container. First of all you will need to trim the foam to the right size and shape using a sharp knife to trim away small sections at a time.

Alternatively, press the opening or base (if it is the same size) of your container down into the block of foam to leave an imprint mark and, using this as your guide, trim the block to fit. The foam should fit snugly inside the container. Then trim the top of the foam into a rounded shape; this allows you to arrange the flowers evenly over the entire surface and angle them at the sides. The foam should always stand about 2.5cm (1 in) above the rim of your container.

3 Foam needs to be secured to your chosen container otherwise the weight of the flowers may tip it over. If you are using a vase, jug or jar, then foam can be cut to fit the neck of your container tightly, just press it in gently and you won't need any extra support.

5 Another way of holding the foam in place is to press it onto a pinholder (fixed to the container with a blob of adhesive clay), making sure that the spikes go all the way in.

6 If you are putting together a large or top-heavy arrangement, you can make doubly sure that your foam is held securely by taping right over the top of it and onto the container with florist's adhesive tape.

The first stem you push into the foam is the most important; it balances the foam for the rest of the arrangement so make sure it is firmly inserted. Don't be tempted to push the stems in too far – about three centimetres, an inch is enough – otherwise they will criss-cross each other and the foam might break up.

2 If you are using green foam for fresh flowers, soak the foam after trimming – but not under running water. Fill a bowl or sink with cold water deeper than the depth of the foam. Hold the foam over the top and gently let go. Don't push it into the water, let it sink slowly down. If you 'dunk' the foam it will

4 Alternatively, if you are using foam in a shallow container, it must be fixed in place with a florist's prong. Secure it to the bottom of the vase with a blob of adhesive clay. This fixative won't stick to a wet surface, so make sure your vase is completely dry inside. (Don't use fixative on your best silver as it will cause tarnishing.) When the prong is stuck down, press the foam gently down into the spikes

Buying & Cutting Flowers

An important part of getting the most from cut flowers is to buy or pick them at the right stage of development. With some flowers, buying them when they are immature is as bad, if not worse, than buying them when they are past their best. It pays to spend extra time selecting the best specimens, particularly if you are choosing expensive, exotic blooms.

As a general rule, aim to buy or cut flowers from your own garden when a few flowers are fully open and there are plenty of buds showing colour. Often, tight green buds will not open once cut.

Some kinds of flowers have special requirements. This is what to look for if you want to be sure of buying blooms that will stay looking good in the vase for as long as possible.

ALSTROEMERIA
Buy when at least one flower has opened and there are plenty of buds showing their true colour.

ANTHURIUM
The palette-shaped flowers should be completely open when you buy them; avoid any that are curled up or brown round the edges.

BOUVARDIA
Buy when some flowers are open and some buds are opening, with the remainder just showing colour.

CARNATION
Cut or buy when the flowers are just open, and the outer petals are still crisp. Avoid buying any specimens with withered or discoloured leaves.

CARTHAMUS
Buy or cut when the colour of the buds can be seen clearly and a few buds on each stem have just started to open.

CHRYSANTHEMUM
Buy spray chrysanthemums when most of the flowers have opened out fully and only the few buds remain. The flower on single stem chrysanthemums should be open but the centre should be tightly packed, indicating that there are more petals open.

CORNFLOWER
Cut or buy when the flowers are fully open but show no fading on the outer petals.

CYMBIDIUM ORCHID
Choose stems of flowers on which all except the top two or three blooms are open. Individual flowers bought separately should be fully open.

DELPHINIUM
Cut or buy when most of the flowers are open, with just a few near the top of the spike still in bud.

DILL
Cut from the garden or buy from the florist when all the flowers are fully open, but none drop off when the bunches are shaken lightly.

ERYNGIUM (SEA HOLLY)
Cut or buy when most of the flowers are fully open.

FREESIA
Buy when the flower at the tip of the spike is open and most of the remaining buds are showing their true colour.

GERBERA
The flowers should be fully open, but look carefully into the centre of each and reject any where the pollen is visible. They will not last as long as younger flowers that have not started to shed pollen.

GLADIOLUS
Cut or buy when the lowest flower has just started to open, the next few are showing their true colour and the rest are tight green buds.

GYPSOPHILA
Examine the flowers closely to see which are open. Only choose stems where more than half the flowers are open but some are still in bud.

IRIS
Buy when the flowers are beginning to unfurl or still in bud, but only if the colour of the flowers is just visible.

LIATRIS
Unlike most spikes of flowers, liatris flowers open from the top downwards. Buy or cut those with a few flowers open at the top of each spike.

LILY
Cut or buy in bud, choosing only those where most buds are showing their true colour and the first flowers are just beginning to open. Buds that are too tightly shut never open.

MICHAELMAS DAISY
Cut or buy when most of the flowers are fully open and a few are at the partly-open bud stage. The flowers last well in water, especially if you lightly crush the stem ends, dip them in boiling water and then stand them in deep, cool water for several hours before arranging them.

MIMOSA
Buy when the flowers are just open, and avoid any that are already shedding pollen. To prolong the vase life and retain the brilliant colour of the flowers, lightly hammer the ends of the stems to enable them to take up water more readily, place them in deep water and cover the flowers with a plastic bag for several hours.

MOLUCELLA
Pick or buy when all the flowers are open and remove the leaves to appreciate fully the spike of green flowers.

NARCISSUS
Cut or buy narcissus and daffodils when the buds are only just beginning to open so that you can enjoy watching the flowers unfold.

NERINE
Pick or buy when the flowers are starting to open; avoid any that are tinged with blue as these will not last long.

PEONY
Cut from the garden or buy when the buds are showing their true colour; if the flowers are open already they won't last in the vase.

POPPY
Pick when the buds are just starting to unroll and seal the stem ends by passing them through a naked flame for a fraction of a second.

ROSE
Buy or cut when the buds are just starting to open – don't buy roses from the florist in very tight bud or the necks may bend and the flowers won't open at all.

RUDBECKIA
Cut when most of the flowers are just opening and a few are fully open.

SCABIOUS
Cut or buy when the buds have opened or are just opening.

SCHIZOSTYLIS
Cut or buy when one or two of the lower

flowers on each spike are open, with plenty of buds further up the stem showing some colour.

STATICE
Cut or buy when most of the florets that make up each head are just open.

SWEET PEA
Cut or buy when the lowest flower on each stem has just opened.

TRACHELIUM
Buy when each flowerhead comprises mostly buds but a few flowers are open.

TULIP
Cut or buy when the flowers are just open, although buds that are showing their full colour and are just starting to open also are acceptable. Avoid tight green buds as they will never open.

Caring for Flowers

When flowers and foliage are cut from the garden or from a pot plant, or brought home from the florists, before arranging them time needs to be spent giving the plant material the necessary treatment to make them last as long as possible when they are arranged in the container. All flowers and foliage benefit from a long drink in a deep bucket which has been almost filled with tepid water. If the flowers have been bought from a flower shop the florist has probably had them in water for a time – but as you do not know how long, there is no harm in making sure by giving them a long drink.

Before placing the flowers in the bucket, the ends of the stems should be treated so that they will take up water more readily. This preparation is necessary because, after the flowers have been cut, the sap at the end of the stem dries quickly and forms a seal. The following treatments should be carried out, both when the flowers are given their initial drink, and also, if you need to re-cut them again, when they are finally arranged. Remember to put the flowers into water immediately after they have been prepared.

Soft stems e.g. tulip, arum lily. These can usually take up water easily. Cut each stem on the slant to give a larger area through which the stem can drink than a straight cut.

Hard and woody stems e.g. roses and lilacs. These have greater difficulty in absorbing water than soft-stemmed flowers and foliage. Make a small slit up the centre of each stem for about 2.5cm (1in). Alternatively, scrape away the outer covering or bark of the lowest 25mm (1 in) of stem or, hammer the end of each woody stem so that the tissues are crushed. Hammering woody stems can be quicker when preparing them for the initial drink, but when cutting them to the required length for an arrangement, it is more convenient to slit or scrape them. Crushed stems are also harder to insert in floral foam, and can quickly pollute the water.

Hollow stems e.g. lupins and delphiniums. Flowers with hollow stems are liable to quickly wilt, and droop their heads. To prevent this, turn each flower upside down over the sink, and with a small watering-can fill the stem with water. Then you can either plug the stem with a small piece of florist's foam or cotton wool and place it in the bucket of tepid water, or you can simply hold your thumb over the bottom of the stem, put it into the water and take your thumb away. The pressure of water in the bucket will keep the stem filled with water. When you cut the stem to the length that the arrangement requires, do this under the water and replace the stopper. If you need to cut a treated stem when it is out of the water, turn it upside down. You can then cut it to the required length without losing water.

Hot water treatment e.g. dahlias and young spring foliage. These plant materials will benefit from the hot water treatment as will flowers which droop after they have been in an arrangement for a day or two; this happens particularly to greenhouse-grown roses. To revive them dip the ends of the stems in boiling water. Bring a pan of water to the boil and place the bottom 2.5cm (1 in) of the stems in the water, having first protected the flower heads from steam by wrapping them in either tissue paper or polythene bags. Leave them in the water for about 20 seconds then take them out and place in tepid water which comes nearly up to their heads.

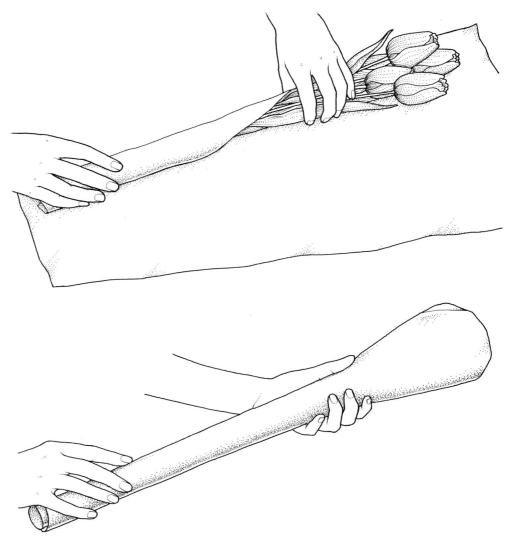

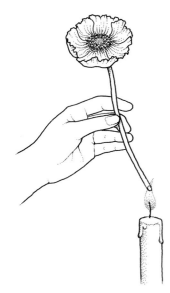

Burning stems e.g. euphorbias and poppies. When these flowers are cut they give off a white milky substance and they are said to be 'bleeding'. Holding the ends of such stems in a match or gas flame for a few seconds will stop the bleeding and they will be able to absorb water more easily.

Pricking the stems e.g. hellebores, tulips and primulas. These flowers will last very much longer if their stems are pricked with a needle just under the flower heads, preventing an air bubble forming and allowing the flower to take up water more freely. Alternatively, slit up the stem about 2.5cm (1 in) on one side, starting 2.5cm from the bottom.

Submerging certain flowers and foliage e.g. young spring foliage, artichoke leaves, violets and hydrangeas. These all benefit if they are completely submerged while being given their initial drink. Violets take in a great deal of water through their petals, and even after submerging them for the first drink, it is advantageous to spray them overhead occasionally in the arrangement. This greatly increases their life in an arrangement.

Straightening flowers eg. tulips. Tulips are not easy flowers to arrange because their stems curve towards the light. The stems can be straightened by rolling them tightly in greaseproof paper and then placing them in deep water.

Encouraging blooming e.g. gladioli and roses. To encourage flowers to open more rapidly, place them in fairly warm water. With gladioli, if the flowers are not opening when required, remove the top two or three buds, so that the flowers lower down the stem will open more quickly, then place them in fairly warm water. Roses can be gently blown into so that they will open slightly quicker.

Before flowers and foliage are arranged, the leaves which will be submerged should be removed. It is interesting to note that certain flowers such as lilac and dahlia normally have all their leaves removed before arranging). If these are left on, the water will quickly smell very unpleasant, but with clean stems it should stay comparatively fresh. It is not usually necessary to change the water once the flowers have been arranged, but if clean water is needed, it should be tepid. The water level in the container holding the flowers should be looked at each day. On the first day it is advisable to look at it night and morning, as flowers take more water when they are first arranged, but afterwards once a day should be sufficient to keep them fresh-looking. When topping up, use tepid water as the water in the container can become fairly warm.

Special Conditioning for Popular Flowers

Anemones
Dip cut ends in boiling water for a few seconds.

Carnations and pinks
Cut at angle between joints.

Chrysanthemums
Scrape or lightly crush stem ends or make a couple of 2.5cm (1 in) slits up the centre of the stems.

Daffodils
Cut stem back to green part and wash sap away under running water.

Dahlias
Dip the stem ends in boiling water. Hollow-stemmed dahlias should have their stems filled and plugged.

Delphiniums
Fill and plug stems.

Gerbera
Place stem ends in boiling water for a few seconds. If stems are limp, place in a tall water-filled container, with the heads supported on chicken wire.

Gladioli
Cut stems under water and re-cut every 4-5 days.

Hydrangeas
Dip stem ends in boiling water for a few seconds, then submerge flower heads in water for several hours. Spray frequently when arranged.

Iris
Re-cut stem ends frequently, removing the lower white section, that doesn't take up water easily.

Lilac
Scrape and crush or split stem ends. Remove all leaves. Dip stem ends of forced lilac in boiling water for a few seconds.

Lilies
Remove lower white portion of stem and lower leaves.

Peonies
Give a long drink of quite hot water.

Poppies
Cut in bud stage and seal stem ends over a flame. This treatment is also said to prevent the colour fading.

Primulas
Cut short stems.

Roses
Scrape, slit or crush stem end. Re-cut stems frequently.

Stocks
Remove excess foliage, place cut end in boiling water for a few seconds.

Sweet peas
Handle as little as possible and put in shallow water about 2.5cm (1 in) deep.

Tulips
Cut back to the green part of the stem and wash sap away. To prevent drooping, wrap bunch tightly in greaseproof paper and immerse in starch solution (one tablespoon of starch to ½ litre water) for four hours.

Violets
Submerge in water for one hour. Spray arrangement frequently, or submerge overnight.

Reviving Flowers

However well you condition your plant material before arranging it, you may still find that certain flowers wilt quickly in the vase. This is usually due to an airlock in the stem. Such air blockages prevent the flower from taking up water efficiently. Unfortunately, airlocks form as soon as a stem is cut from its parent plant, so one of the only effective preventative measures is to re-cut stems as quickly as possible under water. Remove between 2.5-5 cm (1-2 in) from the flower stems depending on how long they have been out of water. In addition, you can stand the flower stem in boiling water for a few minutes to ease the water flow up the stem.

However, once flowers and foliage have begun to wilt there are several methods of reviving them.

Different flower types respond – with varying degrees of success – to different methods of revival. Though, since both heat and strong light are the principal factors that shorten the vase life of cut flowers, a cool room and a position away from direct sunlight is a common requirement during both the conditioning and revival processes.

Tulips, which can quickly lose their upright characteristic and compact form once they are cut, benefit from being wrapped tightly around with newspaper to cover the stems and flowerheads. The bunch should then be placed in a deep container – such as a bucket – of cool water for several hours. If the petals start to unfurl prematurely, you can place a rubber band – not too tightly – over each flower during this reviving drink. And if the stems start to droop, you can arrest this tendency by pricking through each one with a pin, just beneath the flower head. If the stems are too far gone, and do not respond to this treatment, and if their natural curves have no place in your planned arrangement, you can right matters by pushing a stub wire up through the stem from the base, easing it carefully so that it straightens the stem along its entire length.

Pricking hollow stems with a pin is a simple method of releasing trapped air, which you will find useful with many other flower species. To revive Christmas roses, for example, first prick the stems and then submerge the flowers in cool water for several hours. Recut the stem ends under water before arranging the flowers.

The illustrations and steps below, give you more quick and easy pointers to useful revival techniques for different flower types and foliage too.

1 Green foliage can be submerged in water for at least two hours, enabling it to take up water through its leaves as well as the stem. This treatment should not be used on grey foliage as it tends to diminish the colour.

2 Flowerheads lose their natural texture if submerged for long periods of time, so float sturdy blooms such as roses horizontally in water instead. This treatment only works as a short-term measure.

3 Spray-mist delicate, soft-petalled flowerheads with water to increase their water content. This will help delay shrivelling and fading.

4 Insert your flower into a milk bottle or similar vessel of warm water so the head sits on the rim. Soft-stemmed flowers can be immersed to allow the stems to take up water through the full extent of their outer surface.

Containers

Whatever container you use, it should be an integral part of the design, and not simply something capable of holding water and stems. As well as traditional vases, you can use improvised items and with products such as florist's foam on the market, the container does not even have to be able to hold water.

ESSENTIALS

When buying new containers it is worth knowing that the three most useful shapes are a tall cylinder, a wide shallow bowl, and a bowl shape on top of a stem. Apart from the obvious vase, bowl or jug – all of which still have a place in flower arranging – any of the following should be considered: a candlestick, with candle-cup fitted; a china or glass dish; a pie dish; any china or pottery container of any shape; a drinking glass or goblet; a brandy balloon, (especially for a single bloom); a casserole dish; a bottle; an empty tin can, painted or papered on the outside; a fruit bowl, either glass or wooden; a bread basket; a tea or coffee pot; and an egg cup for tiny posies.

PROPORTIONS

Because the container should contribute to the overall effect, it should neither overwhelm the plant material in it, nor be overwhelmed by it. The shape, size and height of the container in relation to the plant material are all very important. As a general guide, it is said that plant material should measure the height and width of the container, plus half as much again. But it is a mistake to be bound absolutely by this and it is probably better to trust the eye. The height and width of the plant material are not the only factors to be taken into consideration when judging proportion; the bulk, colour and density, which contribute to the visual weight, are also important.

HUES

Neutral colours, such as gray, beige, cream, and white show off most plant material to advantage. Bright primary colours are harder to use with a wide range of flower and foliage colours, but almost any colour can be integrated if one or two flowers of the same shade are added to provide the necessary link.

POSITION

Consider the position to be occupied by the arrangement when deciding on the height, shape and colour of the container. For example, an arrangement for a buffet table viewed by people standing up, should be large enough to make an impression, and front facing, to maximize the impact of the flowers you have to work with.

CLEANLINESS

Not only does a clean vase, especially a glass one, look more attractive than a dirty one, cleanliness is important for the cutflowers and foliage, too. Dirty vases encourage the growth of bacteria in the water, causing it to smell foul and become cloudy or discoloured. The bacteria also prevent stems taking up water effectively, thus shortening the life of cut flowers.

Always clean vases after every use, using soap, water and a mild disinfectant. Rinse in fresh water and dry thoroughly before storing.

Antique or other valuable containers may need special treatment.

CONTAINER HINTS

It is possible to transform a collection of flowers into a successful display by selection the right container. A container can have an affect on the colour, texture and mood of the flowers and foliage you have to hand and can dictate the type of display you create.

● Whatever your choice, the neck and size of the container is most important: if the neck of the vase is too wide, the flowers will fall out of position; if too narrow they will look cramped and unnatural.

● Glass containers lend themselves to loose, informal arrangements; they come in all shapes and sizes from vases, bowls and cubes to fish tanks and tiny bottles. Any stem-holding material such as foam or chicken wire looks ugly through clear glass, so the flowers must be allowed to fall naturally in the vase or bowl. The beauty of displaying flowers in glass containers is the pure, fresh look that can be achieved – the colours of the flowers are not in competition with the colour of the vase, and as long as the water is always kept clean and fresh, the natural beauty of the flowers can be appreciated to the full.

● Ceramic containers have a different kind of appeal. From the palest pastels to bright primary colours and earthy terracotta, a ceramic container can be chosen to emphasise or contrast with the colour of the flowers. As ceramic vases are opaque, different display styles can be achieved by using stem-holding material to keep the flowers in place.

● Metal containers are a more unusual choice, and different types of metal have varying effects on the mood of an arrangement. Cold-looking metals such as pewter make the flower colour seem cool, whereas yellow metals such as brass,

copper and bronze lend a warm glow to the flowers.

● Baskets have a rustic appeal and have strong associations with informal, massed arrangements of wild and cottage flowers. A waterproof container such as a small plastic box needs to be placed inside the basket before fresh flowers can be arranged in this kind of container.

● For the best-looking floral displays be inventive and look for the unexpected when choosing the right containers for arrangements. A whole range of household objects make unusual but effective containers for any style of flower design: from chunky kitchen storage jars, casserole dishes and crockery or delicate china teapots to wooden boxes and hollowed-out fruit.

Practical Design

SCALE AND PROPORTION

Scale denotes the size of materials used in an arrangement in relation to each other and their surroundings.

Proportion denotes the quantities of materials used in an arrangement in relation to each other and their surroundings. Scale and proportion are often confused and it may be useful to consider these design principles in terms of the components of an arrangement. A floral design that combines large chrysanthemum blooms with montbretia (a plant with a spike of flowers) for example, is not in scale as the flower sizes are too disparate. This problem is overcome by introducing some spray carnations and spray chrysanthemums, thus linking the two extremes.

The correct proportions for these plant materials arranged in a design can be achieved only if the quantities of each flower type are correct in relation to each other. In this instance, five large chrysan-

themum blooms, nine montbretia spires, five stems of spray chrysanthemums and seven stems of spray carnation. In other words, the number of dominant flowers, such as chrysanthemums, appropriate for this large arrangement would be unsuitable for a smaller design and likewise with the supporting flowers. Hence scale and proportion are both relative terms.

A PLEASING APPEARANCE

Certain displays, such as a table-centre, need equal amounts of plant material while others, such as asymmetrical display, require a material ratio of 2:1 in order to achieve balance and harmony.

The correct use of scale and proportion and location is important in a church pedestal arrangement which incorporates large, bold material. Most churches have high ceilings so a tall design is required to attract the eye. The same display would overpower a room with a low ceiling.

On the other hand, a miniature arrangement in a very small container holding miniature spray roses, gypsophila, and maidenhair fern is suitable for a dressing table or a mantlepiece, as its scale is appropriate for its surroundings.

The size, height and width of an arrangement are dependent on the setting, interpretation, size of the container and the colour, texture and plant material used. Consequently, flowers and materials should be chosen with their intended location in mind. If you only have a small, delicate container, avoid large, heavy flowers, such as dahlias. Instead, choose light and airy flowers, such as Doris pinks.

FASHIONS IN DESIGN

Ideas on the amount of flowers and foliage used in a design vary considerably and follow fashion trends. An abstract design requires very few flowers, whereas a garden tub needs to be filled with many different flowers. The somewhat over-abundant designs of the Victorian age suit the proportions of the furniture and buildings of that period. Today's designs contain less plant material and so are in scale and proportion to their less ornate surroundings.

Some flower arrangements are enhanced by the use of a baseboard or an accessory, such as a figurine. The size of accessories should be proportional to that of the display. In a landscape design, a representational figurine should be in the same scale as if it were life-size.

THE IMPORTANCE OF SCALE

This illustration shows how important it is to judge the scale of a flower arrangement correctly when positioning it in a wall niche.

The arrangement should occupy approximately two-thirds of the area of the niche. If the display is too large, it will appear cramped in relation to its surroundings; if too small, it will become lost visually and this will detract from the design. The open space around the floral display thus contributes to its overall attraction and is as much a part of the finished design as the actual flowers themselves.

ABOVE RIGHT **This miniature display features** Rosa cornelia, *apple blossom, pink and white saxifrage, grevillea fronds and tips and* Hebe pinguifolia pageii.

USING SCALE AND PROPORTION

1 For a miniature display, choose materials of a similar size with the focal flowers slightly larger. Cut a small piece of florist's foam and shape it to fit the miniature container. Ensure that the foam protrudes above the container rim by about 1cm (½ in) to allow for the downward slant of some of the plant material. Form the outline of the display with small sprays of hebe foliage and fronds of grevillea.

2 Add the miniature roses throughout the design to give weight and colour. Although they are the largest blooms, they should not be allowed to dominate the display as this would affect the scale. Place them deep into the foam for depth. Strengthen the display outline with pieces of apple blossom. Keep turning the container as you work, to ensure you achieve an even shape.

3 Cut down the sprays of pink and white saxifrage into individual flowerheads. Use these to fill in any gaps in the arrangement, ensuring that the foam is covered completely. The small, white saxifrage flowers will lighten the display. If you still have gaps in the design, include additional hebe or grevillea. The plant material should be in scale in relation to each other and no particular flower should either dominate the arrangement or appear insignificant.

1

2

3

Practical Design

BALANCE

Balance within a design is the state of equilibrium between all its elements so that none dominates. There are two kinds of balance: actual and visual. Actual, or physical, balance is easy to understand because it simply means that an object is stable and will not fall over. Visual balance is a little more complex. If an object is not balanced visually, it won't necessarily fall over, but it will appear to be top heavy, bottom-heavy or lop-sided. A design that is unbalanced visually will contain elements that detract from the rest of the design.

ACTUAL BALANCE

To achieve actual balance the plant material within a design must be placed correctly to prevent the arrangement from toppling over. Actual balance can be accomplished by mastering the mechanics of flower arranging. If a church pedestal has too many heavy flowers at the top of the design or if it bulges at the front, the arrangement will be in danger of falling. However, if you use holding devices, such as pinholders and florist's foam, and the plant material is placed correctly – with the smallest or most slender material at the top forming the outline and the larger, heavier flowers placed in the heart of the design – physical instability should not arise.

VISUAL BALANCE

A flower arrangement can be balanced physically without being balanced visually. In general, the eye is drawn to the area in a design that is perceived to contain the most interest. The materials in a visually balanced design will be arranged around an imaginary vertical or horizontal axis so the eye is drawn equally to both sides.

Visual balance does not necessarily mean all the material has to be exactly the same either side of the imaginary central axis; such rigid symmetry can make a design monotonous. Instead, both sides of the imaginary axis should have the same visual weight, irrespective of the materials used. For example, it is possible to use foliage, such as a few stems of fern, on one side of a design to establish its width and counterbalance this on the other side with sprays of eucalyptus – in such a design it is the proportions used that provide the key to establish equal visual weight. Therefore, if one side of an arrangement has two or three large stems of plant material, the other side should be counterpoised with several stems of smaller material so that the sides are balanced visually even though they are not symmetrical.

VISUAL INTEREST IN DESIGNS

Visual interest in flower arrangements can derive from colour, texture and shape. The most common cause of visual imbalance is uneven colour distribution. A flower with a strong or advancing colour has more luminosity than the flowers around it and therefore attracts attention to itself. Such advancing colours range from yellow through orange to red. Receding colours, such as blues and violets, do not attract the eye immediately as they lack luminosity and are visually weaker than advancing colours. Green is a neutral shade.

Bold colours should be distributed evenly throughout a flower arrangement. Place large boldly-coloured flowers towards the centre of a design with similarly coloured buds at the top so the outer flowers are anchored visually to the display centre. Avoid placing large, bright flowers on a design outline and blooms in receding colours in the centre as this makes the display appear top heavy and lacking in depth and visual stability.

Visual interest may come from texture. A shiny texture demands more attention than a dull one because of the amount of light reflected and therefore it is important to distribute glossy plant material evenly throughout a display, with the majority positioned within the focal area.

Shape also can determine visual balance. Often plant materials that differ greatly in size and shape need to be balanced. A large feature flower, can be counterbalanced with a group of much smaller flowers, placed higher and to the other side of the design.

LEFT The heavy form of the dog statue on the left-hand side of this display is balanced by the arching foliage to the right.

1 Tape a block of soaked florist's foam to the neck of a tall vase. Use two tiarella spikes placed to one side of the foam to set the height of the display. Use three to four arching Solomon's seal sprays to balance the height and establish the width by positioning them pointing outwards and downwards on the right-hand side. Strengthen the outline with safari foliage. Position two or three hosta leaves at the base to add visual weight.

2 Create the central focal area of colour with a line of three lilies. Their size and advancing colour help balance the display and the line of flowers echoes the outline of the arrangement, preventing the design from appearing to tilt to one side. Fill in with alstroemeria, making sure that the design does not appear too crowded or lose its shape.

3 Group spray carnations to the front left-hand side of the display to counterbalance the long line of the alstroemeria and the polygonium. Use small sprays of safari foliage to cover any exposed areas of foam. Although the completed design is not symmetrical, it is balanced both actually and visually.

LEFT An asymmetrical display using lilic tiarella, alstroemeria, spray carnations, Solomon's seal, hosta and safari foliage.

Practical Design

DOMINANCE AND CONTRAST

Dominance is the way in which one element of a design attracts attention in preference to another. Contrast is opposition within a design brought about by the dissimilarity of its parts. Dominance and contrast are essential to successful flower arrangements. Dominant flowers provide a focal point that attracts the eye naturally, thus avoiding the monotony created when elements have equal attraction. Dominance involves subordination: a design element can only appear dominant in contrast with other supporting elements.

Contrast emphasises the differences in the plant materials used in an arrangement; variation is a mild form of contrast. Contrast can be introduced into a design through diversity of colour, texture, form and style. Dominance and contrast are very closely allied as a good design uses contrast to support and emphasise its dominant element.

DOMINANCE IN FLOWER DISPLAYS

Before embarking upon a flower arranging project, decide which element you wish to dominate; usually this will be some of the plant material. For example, in a traditional triangle comprising roses, larkspur, syringa, and lady's mantle blooms and elaeagnus and hosta foliage, the roses will be the dominant feature as they are larger and denser than the other ingredients. The other plant material is visually subordinate, but is important to the overall design to provide contrast.

The dominant feature in a flower arrangement does not have to be the plant material. In early Chinese and Egyptian displays, emphasis was placed deliberately on the container. However, in today's designs containers usually play a subordinate role, although attention can be drawn to a particularly beautiful vase.

Accessories, such as bases and drapes, should be subordinate. Consequently, it is best to use accessories in neutral or receding colours, such as beige, grey and soft green or pastel colours, as these will not compete for attention with the plant material or container. Extremely strong colours should be avoided unless the plant material itself is a particularly strong or vivid colour.

If dominance is used correctly, you can avoid the monotony of a design that features equal dimensions, weight of colour or attraction. Use materials to create dynamism and excitement within a design through the inequality of using more dominant than subordinate blooms. This is achieved by introducing a group of strongly coloured flowers into a bunch of more subtle flowers.

Colour has a marked influence on a flower's ability to dominate a design. For example, white attracts the eye more than any other colour and so provides natural emphasis. It is best used in the centre or interspersed throughout an arrangement; if used on the edge it will draw the eye away from the other flowers.

Consequently, always team a white container with at least two or three stems of white plant material, otherwise the eye will be drawn to the vase before the flowers.

USING CONTRAST FOR EFFECT

Contrast can be used to add vitality in flower arrangements. It can be introduced in many different ways: by contrasting rough and smooth textures; shiny and dull surfaces; vertical and horizontal lines; simple and ornate flowers; or a variety of shapes and colours.

Contrast is seen clearly in abstract and modern designs as these emphasise texture and form more than traditional designs which rely on variation rather than clear contrast.

Nature offers many contrasting materials that can be incorporated into many flower designs. For example, in a landscape design, choose contrasting materials, such as matt-textured moss and shiny stones, rough brown bark and cones and light-green, smooth trails of ivy, all of which are associated in nature and also provide contrast in form, texture and colour.

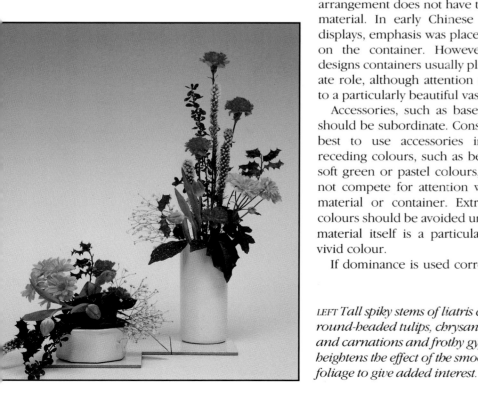

LEFT Tall spiky stems of liatris contrast with round-headed tulips, chrysanthemums and carnations and frothy gypsophila heightens the effect of the smooth-textured foliage to give added interest.

1 Soak a circular foam block and place on a round tray. Position two tall irises and phormium leaves slightly off-centre with two stones at the base. Add two ficus leaves and two schefflera florets low in the foam. Bind small bundles of corn stalks with florists tape and ease them into the front right of the foam at right angles to the display. Add small groups of silver brunia.

2 Place a vertical line of five red roses to the left of the display, staggering their heads. Balance these with a single rose placed low to the right. Cluster four or five ears of corn together and place to the right of the display to contrast with the horizontal line of the stalks. Cover the front of the foam with about 20 plastic cherries for colour dominance.

3 Add white erica and spray chrysanthemums to the right-hand side of the display in colour groupings as a contrast to the strong red of the roses. Finish the design by adding groups of reindeer moss and golden mushrooms to contrast with the smooth, shiny surface of the ficus and schefflera leaves.

LEFT Here, tall foliage and red roses and cherries dominate the display through tone and shape while the subordinate material adds textural contrast.

Practical Design

HARMONY

Harmony is the accord or unity between the elements of a design that make it appear an artistically pleasing whole. Harmony is not necessarily a separate design principle as it is largely the result of the successful application of the other principles we have covered in previous issues: balance, scale and proportion, rhythm and repetition, and dominance and contrast. When these are applied correctly, and each element of a design is related to the other parts, harmony will have been achieved.

The relationship of each element in a design to the other parts is important to the design's overall harmony; none of the elements should be in conflict with the others or with the overall design, except as deliberate contrast. This relationship may be in a similarity of colour, texture, shape or style. Often it is easiest to achieve a relationship between elements which are associated in nature. For example, for a sea-inspired display, choose materials and accessories associated with the sea, such as shells or a piece of fishing net. The addition of woodland moss would be disharmonious as it is not associated with the seashore.

HARMONY IN ARRANGEMENTS
Harmony is easier to achieve in simple designs which include a few well-chosen plant materials rather than complicated designs which may end up looking fussy. Often elaborate designs contain so many elements competing for attention that it is impossible to gain a clear sense of purpose from the overall design. It is a measure of a good design that if you remove one element the design will seem incomplete or, if you add material, the design will appear over-elaborate.

A good design should be perfectly in keeping with its setting so that the style and plant materials used reflect the colour, style, size and period of the display's final location. For example, a rustic landscape-style arrangement would seem inappropriate in a Regency drawing room, whereas it would be entirely in harmony with a country-style kitchen.

Repetition of colour, shape, texture or style is an easy and effective way of achieving harmony. It can be used to link separate design elements together to achieve unity. For example, combine black-centred red gerberas with a black vase to unify the combination of plant material and container.

DISPLAY CONTAINERS
Containers have a direct influence on the harmony of a design. A container always should be linked to the plant material it holds by shape, colour or style. For example, if a container is strongly coloured, some of the flowers should repeat that colour. Likewise, if you are using very delicate flowers, such as orchids, roses or gypsophila, a glass or silver container would be the most appropriate vessel.

INTEGRATING COMPONENTS
Accessories and drapes are among the most difficult elements to integrate successfully into a flower display. In general, accessories should be included only if they are absolutely right for the design. For example, a very elaborate china figurine would not harmonise with a basket of dried flowers. Drapes also can look incongruous if not used discerningly as they are completely unsuitable for many flower arranging styles, especially modern designs. They look best in a toning colour with a traditional design.

USING BASEBOARDS
Bases can present similar difficulties because often it is not possible to match bases to a particular flower arranging style. Although a dainty display of velvet-textured pansies intended for a formal setting would be in harmony with a velvet baseboard, if the same arrangement were placed on a raffia mat or a piece of wood, the harmony would be lost and the display split visually into two parts. However, display the pansies on a table set for an informal meal, and a raffia mat would be in keeping with the flowers.

LEFT This traditional, triangular arrangement is unified by the shades. Even the copper-toned container harmonizes with the wonderful golden hues of the flowers and foliage.

USING HARMONY

1 Immerse half a block of florist's foam in water and place it inside a delicate china container. Place aquilegia foliage around the edge of the container to establish the width of the arrangement and add three stems of tiny-flowered bleeding heart to set the height. Add three short sprays of white lilac blossom, one positioned in the centre and one either side of the display. Ensure that the container is not obscured as it forms an integral part of the design.

2 Cut eight to ten roses to graduated lengths and add so that they form a diagonal line across the display. Position lily of the valley and wallflowers evenly throughout the arrangement to build up the dome shape. Recess some of the larger blooms slightly. These dainty focal flowers complement the ornate, delicate container.

3 Finally, add small sprays of forget-me-not and gypsophila throughout the display as light filler flowers. The colour and style of the flowers have been chosen to reflect the china bowl and so unify plants and container.

LEFT Small garden flowers – bleeding heart, lilac blossom, forget-me-not, wallflower, roses and gypsophila – are chosen to harmonize with the soft shades and delicate style of this china bowl.

$\mathscr{T}$RADITIONAL TECHNIQUES

A flower arrangement depends for its appeal on the beauty of its flowers, but also on the way in which it is put together. Good composition can transform modest raw material into an impressive display; sloppy composition can detract from even the loveliest blooms.

An arrangement can be front-facing, backed by a wall and seen, like a painting, from one position only; or 'all-round', to be viewed from every angle, like a sculpture. Front-facing displays are popular for buffet tables and sideboards; all-round displays are ideal for dining-room tables and coffee tables.

An arrangement can be formal, following a chosen geometric form, such as a triangle, circle or curve; or informal, as if just bunched in the hand and transferred to a vase. Informal displays still need careful thought, and many beginners find it easier to start with formal arrangements, because of their precise guidelines and proportions. Once you become more experienced, you may prefer creating displays that fall between the two, with a roughly geometric outline, but relaxed in feeling.

A MATTER OF TASTE

The colour wheel theory on pp 58-59 sets out the relationship between the primary colours (red, yellow and blue) and the secondary colours (green, purple and orange) of the spectrum. The theory helps you predict which colours will look restful or lively together but in fact, you soon learn to trust your own judgement.

As a rule of thumb, monochromatic schemes, based on variations of a single colour – say, from pale pink to deepest red – are 'safe' and pleasing to look at. So, too, are all-white schemes, and monochromatic schemes with white added. Two-colour (bi-colour) schemes; and multi-colour (polychromatic) ones range from harmonious to contrasting, depending on choice of colours. Pink and pale blue, for example, convey a peaceful feeling, while bright blue and orange convey a lively, excited one. Though sharply contrasting colours may be overwhelming used on a large scale, flower arrangements that are relatively small, and a bright concentration of colour may be just what a room needs. Don't be afraid to experiment! You will soon discover just what you find pleasing and will learn to trust your own taste.

PLANNING THE DESIGN

When composing a design, however formal or informal, in which the shape of the plant material plays an important role, making a sketch plan of it first may help you to visualize a successful display. Draw in the outline shape of the container and the shape and proportions of the principal stems – a crescent of cascading broom, a shower of ivy trails, or the straight, tall stems of gladioli. Once you see the sketch on paper, it will be easier to select the most appropriate material, position correctly and this provides the framework for the other 'filler' flowers.

GENERAL TIPS

● An all-round display is easiest to start with, since you just fill in an imaginary sphere with flowers, radiating from a single point. When creating an all-round display, always turn it as you proceed, so it is equally dense and attractive all over.

● When choosing a colour scheme, remember the foliage as well as the flowers. It is often green, but can also be gold, white, purple or silvery grey. Remember, too, the container's colour, which is an inherent part of the display.

● Choose colours with the setting in mind. If you need inspiration, wallpaper, upholstery, curtains or carpets can offer a wealth of ideas. Patterned fabrics and papers are especially helpful, since they provide a ready-made scheme. A room with a neutral colour scheme, such as white, beige or grey is like a blank canvas, and any floral colours are suitable.

● Try seasonal colours: pastels, especially yellow and blue, in spring; multi-colours in summer; golds and oranges in late summer or autumn; and Christmas red and green in winter.

● If you're a beginner, start by restricting yourself to one variety of flower, as shown on pages 44-57. It helps you concentrate on composition, and still achieve attractive finished results. Once you are comfortable doing single-variety displays, gradually build up the number of different varieties you include.

● Always allow for sufficient space around the completed arrangement, so it doesn't look awkward or cramped.

Classic Forms

Everything we see and touch has a shape or form. Leaves vary in shape, from the long, pointed blades of gladioli and iris, to triangular ivy and arum and rounded geranium and bergenia. Flower shapes range from slender sprays of blossom to spries of delphiniums, bell-shaped lilies and rounded chrysanthemums and roses. These shapes can be described in geometric terms such as straight lines, circles, triangles and square lines, in terms of three-dimensional forms: tubes, spheres, pyramids and cubes.

Larger shapes and forms are created once flowers and leaves are arranged in a container. In spite of the sprays and tendrils which protrude from the mass, the outline is often roughly geometric.

The basic, or classic, geometric forms can be divided into groups: those based on straight lines, angles and triangles; and those which are curved and circular. In addition, these forms may be symmetrical, with each side of the central backbone the identical reverse of the other in outline; or asymmetrical with dissimilar units on either side.

Two primary factors tend to influence the type of form used: personal taste and the place chosen to display the arrangement. In addition, the type of plant material available also governs form – curving shapes may need some curved stems and long straight stems suggest tall vertical displays.

SYMMETRICAL FORMS

Symmetrical triangles range from the tall and narrow (sometimes called 'vertical') to the low and squat – 'horizontal'. The 'vertical' triangle is elegant and suitable for a tall narrow space; its height particularly suits a modern decor. If the display is stable, use the vertical triangle as a buffet table decoration; it takes up little space and presents the flowers at eye-level when guests are standing at the table. For a seated meal, the 'horizontal' triangle allows easy conversation across the table. Decorative candles in toning colours can be used in the arrangement as the flowers and leaves will be low and therefore present no fire hazard. Low triangles also are suitable for a coffee table, where the

ABOVE *One of the most distinctive and classic arranging styles is the Hogarth curve which follows a definite 'S' shape. This gives an arrangement a pleasing outline.*

flowers are seen from above.

Large pedestal arrangements and smaller displays raised in containers are often symmetrical triangles. Such displays tend to be higher than they are wide, and therefore need straight, relatively long stems to form their backbone, as well as longer placements within the display.

Oval and circular arrangements, both formal and informal, also are symmetrical, and look best placed below eye level, especially on tables on where they can be seen from all angles. Cone and sphere shapes are also symmetrical and look very effective given all-round space but if preferred they can be viewed from the front alone, as when placed on a mantelpiece.

ASYMMETRICAL FORMS

While symmetrically balanced designs are perhaps the simplest forms to create in flower arrangements, asymmetrical lines offer scope for less rigid and more exciting displays. The asymmetrical triangle is often used in flower arranging competitions and allows for the use of an accessory, such as a figurine, plate, bottle or fan, which helps emphasise chosen subject. Pairs of asymmetrical arrangements are often used either side of a mantelpiece, rather like decorative bookends.

HOGARTH CURVES

Crescent shapes and curves can be symmetrical or asymmetrical and often incorporate curved stems such as broom for outlines. The Hogarth curve, which is two continuous 'C' curves with one reversed, was called the 'line of beauty' by William Hogarth, the 18th-century painter, who used it for the 'G' in his signature. Hogarth curves need a tall container, or a raised one, such as a candlestick fitted with a candlecup, so that the plant material can flow downwards as well as upwards. A Hogarth curve can be arranged vertically or diagonally, when it is sometimes called a 'Lazy S'. Of all geometric-based floral displays, the Hogarth curve creates a sense of movement.

As the outlines of the Hogarth and other curved arrangements depend for their grace and form on the shapes and positioning of the principal stems, it is important to select these with particular care. If you cannot find stems with suitable curves, it is possible to induce the desired shape in supple stems such as broom, winter jasmine, honeysuckle or clematis. To do this soak stems in water, coil them into a circle, then tie them with twine and leave them for two or three hours. At the end of this time the stems should have adopted just the gently curving lines you need for "C", "S" and other curved designs.

RIGHT The strong distinctive style of the Hogarth curve is seen again in this arrangement. Placing such a dramatic display against a dark background accentuates its form.

Classic Triangle

A TRIANGULAR SHAPED ARRANGEMENT TO CREATE AN IMPRESSIVE WELCOME FOR VISITORS. THIS ARRANGEMENT IS AN EXAMPLE OF A FORMAL DISPLAY THAT USES TRADITIONAL PRINCIPLES

Traditional flower arranging goes back to Edwardian, or even Georgian, times, when huge, generous displays of garden, greenhouse and wild flowers, loosely arranged into oval, bouquet-like bunches, filled English country and suburban houses. In the late 1940s and 1950s, the geometry became more pronounced and stylized, with tighter, more controlled displays replacing exuberant ones. The arrangement shown here combines the obvious geometry of a symmetrical tri-angle with the relaxed generosity of earlier Edwardian times.

CHOOSING THE FLOWERS

No one flower is dominant in this theme, and though the combination used here is especially attractive, other flowers could be substituted. It can be based entirely on garden flowers, a mixture of garden and florist flowers or, as here, florist flowers alone. Some flowers symbolize certain times of the year: the distinctly wintery

Euphorbia fulgens used here, for example, and spring-like hyacinths. By changing the flowers within the same basic structure you could create summer or autumn displays. For a summer arrangement lilacs would aptly replace the hyacinths, and arching sprays of white bridal wreath, the euphorbia.

The colour theme here is pink, with touches of blue. It avoids being 'sugary sweet' by ranging the shades and tints of each colour from fresh to subtle and smoky. You could substitute a cream and white theme; or a yellow, apricot and orange one, with perhaps rich brown glycerined beech foliage instead of the blue foliage used here.

Large-flowered Dutch hyacinths are chosen for their delicious fragrance as well as their bright pink colour. Buy hyacinths when the florets are showing colour, and have started to open, but before they're fully open, to get the maximum display life of about a week. If the stems are twisted

when you buy them, carefully and tightly wrap the bunch in newspaper, then soak it in a deep bucket or jug of cool water for several hours, or overnight.

FLOWERS FOR ARCHING SPRAYS

Euphorbia fulgens, a tender relative of poinsettia, garden spurges and 'crown of thorns' house plant, provides arching sprays of tiny pink flowers and eucalyptus-like, blue-grey leaves. It is available in late autumn and winter; buy stems with most of the flowers open, and handle gently. You will probably have to order it from your florist; if unavailable, use arching sprays of eucalyptus instead.

Standard fringed carnations, with their heavily-cut petals, are more graceful than ordinary, large-flowered types, which have a dense, massive appearance. However, solid pink carnations are suitable and they are more widely available. Whichever you choose, buy them half open, for the longest display life.

Single-flowered 'de Caen' anemones are featured, but you could use double-flowered forms instead, or even single pink chrysanthemums. Pink-red anemones are ideal, but you may have to buy two bunches of mixed colours, and extract the

SEALING EUPHORBIA STEMS

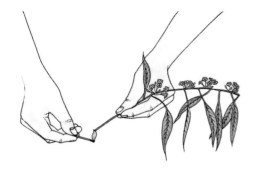

Euphorbia stems exude a milky latex when cut. This sticky fluid can block the stem, preventing it from absorbing water, and can also harm other flowers in the display. It is worse in vases of water than in foam blocks, where individual stems are more isolated. To seal a stem, hold a lighted match to the end for a few seconds, or dip it briefly in boiling water. The latex gives some people a skin rash, so handle euphorbia with care. If you get latex on your skin, wash it off at once; if euphorbia has given you a rash before, wear rubber gloves when handling it. It is also important to keep latex out of your eyes, because it is such an irritant.

CREATING YOUR FORMAL FRONT-FACING DISPLAY

INGREDIENTS

1 *6 hyacinth stems*
2 *20 anemones*
3 *13 fringed carnations*
4 *12 blue trachelium stems*
5 *10 pink euphorbia stems*

6 *12 stems (from one branch) of blue fir*
7 *block of florist's foam*
8 *prong and adhesive clay*
9 *florist's knife*
10 *china pedestal vase*

1 Attach a prong to a pedestal vase, with adhesive clay. Saturate a foam block, then cut it to fit, and fix it on the prong. Divide one branch of blue fir into 12 sprigs, 15-20cm (6-8 in) long, then remove the lower needles. Evenly space nine sprigs horizontally around the sides of the block and three upright sprigs in the centre.

4 Strip the lower half of ten euphorbia stems of leaves and flowers, to allow maximum water to reach the remaining foliage and flowers. Distribute the arching branches in a ten-pointed, star-shaped pattern, with the rear branches upright; the side branches, horizontal; and the longest branches arching downwards in the front.

2 Snip the ends off six hyacinth stems, cutting straight across, not at an angle, and varying the stem lengths from 10cm (4 in) to full size. Insert the stems in the centre of the block, holding them at the bottom or they will bend or snap. Try not to leave hyacinth stems out of water for long, as they quickly lose their moisture content and wilt.

3 Snip the ends off 13 carnations, varying the heights. Cut between the bumps (nodes), so the stems can take up water. Use the tallest four stems to set the display's height, placing them behind the hyacinths. Use seven more to form a horizontal cluster to one side of the display and group two on the other side.

pink flowers. In that case, choose bunches with the most pink, or pink and cream blooms. Don't waste the scarlet and purple ones – use them in another arrangement, or display them alone, in a tall glass tumbler. Anemone stems, like hyacinths, can twist; so straighten them carefully, as you did with the hyacinth stems.

The most unusual floral ingredient is the trachelium, or throatwort. A member of the *Campanula* family, trachelium resembles sedum, with its flat heads of tiny, lavender blue flowers. Sedum could be substituted, especially in an autumnal arrangement, when russet-red tones are needed. Both are suitable for drying. Trachelium can be grown in the garden, and although perennial, is often treated as a half-hardy annual.

CHOOSING THE FOLIAGE
Blue fir, or *Abies procera* provides the foliage for this display. Its branches are densely covered with stiff blue needles, and sprigs of it are excellent for adding bulk to a display, without adding the sombre tones usually associated with conifer foliage.

Blue fir is available from florists, but is hardy, so you could cut a small branch from a tree growing in the garden. If you want to plant one to supply you with foliage all year round, choose the variety 'Glauca', which is a beautiful silvery-blue. For this display, you could also use blue-grey juniper or pine, or dark-green spruce foliage.

CHOOSING THE CONTAINER
You need a stemmed container for this display, to allow the euphorbia branches to arch. Here, a simple white-glazed pedestal vase is used, but you could use a plain china or glass cake stand instead. If you do, fix the florist's foam block onto a shallow plastic base, then attach the base to the cake stand with florist's adhesive tape. Then you can water the display, without risking spills.

5 Strip off any lower leaves from 12 trachelium stems. Snip the ends, varying the lengths, then fill out an imaginary triangular frame. Use short-stemmed blooms to build up the density in the middle, and use the tallest ones to reinforce the vertical carnations. Angle a few downwards in the front side of the foam block.

6 Snip the stems of 20 anemones, varying the lengths, but leaving most stems in bud long and cutting those with more open flowers shorter. Put fully open blooms in the centre, to build up visual weight and interest, and use the long-stemmed buds to fill out the triangle's outer points. Check the display from the front and make any final adjustments.

CHOOSING THE SETTING
This is a front-facing display so it looks most attractive with its back against a wall. An ideal location would be on a hall table.

Dome Display

THIS IS AN IDEAL TABLE DISPLAY FOR A COFFEE MORNING. ITS CONVENIENT LOW SHAPE ALLOWS ROOM FOR CUPS,
WHILE PROVIDING A BRIGHT FLORAL POINT TO IMPRESS YOUR GUESTS

A domed display, such as this one, with a collar of foliage round its base, is called a Biedermeier. Named after a style popular in 19th-century Germany, Biedermeiers are based on the idea of a hand-held bunch of flowers. They are classic enough to fit into any decor, simple enough for anyone to make, and can be scaled up or down, according to your budget and the available space in the chosen room.

CHOOSING THE FLOWERS
Two bunches of deep pink tulips are used, but you could use other shades if prefered. Buy them when the buds are shut, but showing colour, and re-cut the stems when you get them home, followed by a long drink of water.

One bunch of blue hyacinths is called for in this arrangement. Buy them when the lowest florets are showing colour, but the top buds are tightly closed, and they will last for a week. Condition hyacinths by re-cutting the stems straight across and giving them a long drink of water.

The kaffir lily, or schizostylis, is the 'odd-flower-out' in this display, since its natural flowering season is autumn. Buy them from the florist when one or two of the lower flowers on each stem are showing colour and beginning to open. A deep-pink variety is shown here, but for a softer effect, choose a pale-pink kaffir lily.

Pink lilies are year-round favourites, but their main season is spring and summer. Buy lilies with all their buds showing colour, but not more than one flower open. When you get them home, cut off the lower, white portion of the stems, and give them a long drink. Be careful of the dust-like lily pollen; some people prefer to carefully snip off the stamens, so the pollen doesn't stain clothes or furnishings. Creamy-yellow spray carnations, rimmed in red, add a festive touch. Try to buy a bunch with half the flowers open, half in bud, and avoid bunches that have yellow lower leaves and stems.

CREATING A BIEDERMEIER SHAPE

1 Create the symmetrical outline of the display by positioning the stems of leather leaf fern around the outside edge of the florist's foam. Place a few sprigs in the centre as a site for the first flowers. Alternatively, use a few fronds of a Boston fern houseplant.

2 Place the hyacinth stems in a cluster in the centre to set the height of the dome, and the focal point of the design. Place some of the carnations at right angles to the hyacinths around the outside, then begin to fill out the dome shape by angling the others upwards.

3 The symmetrical dome effect is achieved by placing flowers of different lengths throughout the display and angling them at varying degrees to 'round-off' the arrangement. Turn the display to check the shape is consistent from every angle.

SIX STEPS TO A COFFEE TABLE DISPLAY

INGREDIENTS
1 3 stems of laurustinus
2 leafless twigs
3 10 stems of pink tulips
4 5 stems of red and yellow spray carnations
5 4 stems of pink lilies
6 1 bunch of kaffir lilies
7 1 stem of grevillea
8 2 stems of leather leaf fern
9 5 blue hyacinth stems
10 florist's foam
11 shallow, round ceramic bowl
12 florist's knife

1 Fill the bowl a third full of water and secure the wet florist's foam. Insert the leather leaf fern around the outside of the foam to form a collar of foliage. Cut two hyacinth stems to 15cm (6 in) and three to 10cm (4 in), and place them in the centre of the foam. Cut hyacinths straight across and place them in the foam immediately.

4 Trim the kaffir lily stems to about 15cm (6 in), leaving a few leaves near the top. Insert the flowers throughout the arrangement, varying the stem lengths to fit into the overall shape. These tiny flowers give bright splashes of colour to the whole display. The kaffir lily is sensitive to ethylene gas, so keep it away from fruit and vegetables.

2 Define the outline of the display using the carnations. Trim the stems to 12-15cm (5-6 in) and remove most of the foliage. Place some of the stems at right-angles to the hyacinths, at intervals between the fern. Insert the other stems at varying angles, building up a dome shape, and making sure the display is fairly symmetrical.

3 Intersperse the laurustinus with the carnations, reinforcing the rounded outline by angling the foliage towards the centre. Cut the lilies very short (just below the flowerheads) and discard the foliage. Place a few near the hyacinths in the centre, and at various intervals throughout the arrangement, following the dome-shaped frame.

CHOOSING THE FOLIAGE

A mixture of dark-green and brighter foliage adds contrast and helps to hide the florist's foam base. If the types shown here are not available, aim for a variety of leaf shapes and include some dark-green foliage. Leather leaf is a lacy flat florist's fern, traditionally used for collars round the base of Biedermeiers.

Laurustinus is a hardy evergreen shrub, worth growing for year-round foliage for flower arranging. The dark-green foliage adds bulk to arrangements, and provides a cool backdrop for more vivid material. In this display, its pretty, pink-white flowers are a bonus.

Florists sometimes stock laurustinus, but you may have to order it in advance. You could also use elaeagnus or even bay foliage from the garden, or sprigs of florist's eucalyptus.

Slender, colourful grevillea leaves add an unusual touch. Grevilleas are Australian shrubs, too tender for growing outdoors in cool temperate climates. To get the same effect, use a few leaves from a narrow-leaved variety of croton, instead. Finally, leafless twigs are included to break up the outline of the display, and add vertical, contrast to the rounded flower forms.

CHOOSING THE SETTING

The container plays a secondary role in this display, being almost entirely hidden by ferns. When making a Biedermeier you can use a plastic container, though a china one always feels nicer to work with and being heavier, is more stable than a light plastic one.

A coffee table is one of the natural focal points in a living room. Placed in front of the sofa, or in the corner of an 'L'-shaped arrangement of two sofas, a coffee table is where your eye rests naturally. As coffee tables are low, you can also look down on the display, and enjoy its rounded form from above.

Low wooden pedestals on small round wine tables are also ideal for displaying an eye-catching Biedermeier arrangement – literally putting this classic dome display on a pedestal. The shape of the pedestal or table top forms an effective frame for the arrangement's jagged outlines.

5 Remove the leaves from most of the tulips (using a sharp knife). Trim the stems quite short – 12-15cm (5-6 in) – and place them at intervals in the display. Retain some of the cut-off tulip leaves, curve them around your finger and insert them around the outside of the display to add extra texture and shape.

6 Break one stem of grevillea down into several small stems. Curl some of the leaves over and dot them throughout the display; leave others straight so that they stand higher than the flowers. Insert the twigs, snipping them slightly longer to soften the rigid dome shape. Water the display regularly using a small watering can.

Asymetrical arrangement

THIS DISPLAY HAS AN ASYMMETRICAL DESIGN, IDEAL FOR ENHANCING THE BEAUTY
OF FRESH SPRING FLOWERS

Another popular classic shape is the asymmetrical triangle, shown here. The featured display is a perfect foil (accompaniment) for a favourite figurine or any other attractive ornament. It is the addition of the ornamental figurine in this display which makes it more than just another classic formal arrangement. If the flower and ornament are chosen carefully your arrangement can also look as unusual and stylish as the one featured here.

Displays based on an asymmetrical triangle, such as this one, are by their very nature front facing. As with most front-facing displays, this one uses flowers in graduating heights. Each flower stem is a little shorter than the one behind it. Arranged in this way, each flower is clearly visible from the front, so you can appreciate the full value of the symmetry, texture, colour and fragrance of the bloom.

FLOWERS IN PASTEL SHADES
The flowers seen here are available during and after the Christmas period. The colour scheme consists of shades of apricot, peach, pink and white, but one based on lemon or soft rose-pink would be equally nice. Most flowers available in winter have no scent and the ones featured here are no exception, apart from the miniature roses which have only a faint fragrance.

White gerberas, also called Transvaal or Barberton daisies, are the most eye-catching flowers in the display. These are available all year round in a rainbow of colours, ranging from pure white to deep, rich red and purple. They are sold by the stem, and, if well conditioned and looked after, last for at least ten days. As with many daisy-like flowers, avoid using blooms with obvious signs of pollen in the centre – it means that they are already mature and

much of their useful life is over.

Large, standard peach-coloured carnations contrast in shape and colour with the gerberas. Available all year round, carnations come in a wide range of colours, and are sold by the stem.

AN ELEGANT TOUCH
Spray chrysanthemums, or 'mums', as they are called in the trade, in an apricot hue are used to link the peach tones of the carnations and the yellow of the gerbera centres. With their smaller, more delicate blooms, they are useful for filling gaps and allowing the arrangement to maintain an airy feel as they help to prevent the heavy, stolid appearance that displays containing only large flowers sometimes have. When you buy your chrysanthemums, choose a bunch with no more than half the flowers open so you get a longer-lasting display.

Miniature roses are not widely available and you may have to ask your florist to order them for you. They combine the elegance of hybrid tea roses with the dainty charm of smaller roses, such as the old-fashioned favourite, 'Dorothy Perkins'. Pink roses are used here but, again, colour choice depends on availability and your own taste.

VERSATILE EVERGREEN FOLIAGE
Eucalyptus, or gum tree, is among the most versatile of florist's foliage. Its delicately aromatic, blue-grey foliage is long lasting when fresh, but you can also use it dried.

Though there are hundreds of species in the wild, most are semi-hardy and only a few are grown commercially, for the cut foliage. The cider gum, *Eucalyptus gunnii*, with small, rounded leaves is used in this display, but you could also use the spinning gum, *E. perriniana*, with disc-shaped leaves encircling the branches and shoots.

KEEPING YOUR FLOWERS FRESH

A carnation stem, whether of a standard or a spray type, swells to form little bumps, (nodes), where the leaves are attached. The nodes can't take up water as effectively as the rest of the stem so always cut between these nodes, not directly on them. Rose-buds will wilt quickly if picked while still green or if the stems are allowed to become blocked. You can help prevent this by buying only buds showing colour and by re-cutting the stems frequently.
Gerbera stems block quickly once cut. To help keep the flowers fresh, re-cut the stems every three or four days. Adding a drop of bleach to the water also helps. If they do start to wilt, re-cut the stem and then put them in a deep vase of water for 12 hours.

SIX STEPS TO A FRONT-FACING ASYMMETRICAL ARRANGEMENT

1 Fix the bowl to the tray with florist's adhesive clay. Set the display's height with a 45cm (18 in) eucalyptus spray, placed vertically in the middle. Insert smaller sprigs at an angle and horizontally. Let some sprigs overhang the tray, and build up the right-hand side.

4 Remove the lower leaves from the miniature rose stems. Insert the roses in the top and sides of the foam block, varying their heights by angling the stems and inserting them to different depths. Use the longest roses horizontally to emphasise the 'leg' of the display.

INGREDIENTS

1 5 white gerberas
2 5 large peach-coloured carnations
3 3 apricot spray chrysanthemums
4 bunch of pink miniature roses
5 good bunch of eucalyptus sprays
6 small figurine or statuette
7 knife
8 small rectangular tray
9 scissors
10 florist's foam taped to a shallow plastic bowl

2 Cut one chrysanthemum a bit shorter than the main eucalyptus spray and insert it next to the eucalyptus. Insert a carnation with a slightly shorter stem to the right of the 'mum', then insert a shorter gerbera in the centre, left of the 'mum'.

3 Cut a second chrysanthemum stem to the height of the gerbera. Insert the 'mum' stem to the right of the gerbera and under the carnation, to build up the width. Insert a carnation next, between the chrysanthemum and gerbera. Move the eucalyptus to hide the stems of the flowers.

5 Add a shorter gerbera to the right. Cut a third carnation to nearly the full length of the horizontal eucalyptus and insert it at the same angle. Pull off the leafy shoots from the cut-off stem and insert these into the foam block to add bulk and contrast.

6 Insert a short gerbera, at the base. Divide a 'mum' into sprigs and fill in the right-hand side. Insert a gerbera to create a diagonal between the two lowest gerberas. Add two carnations to frame the lowest gerbera. Add the figurine, then use gerbera as a 'bunny tail'.

Tasmanian blue gum, *E. globulus*, with pointed leaves, or silver dollar *E. cinerea*, also with rounded leaves. You can buy eucalyptus by the branch, or in bunches. Try to select branches well furnished with side shoots to give interest to the main vertical outline.

To get the longest-lasting display out of eucalyptus, make sure you cut 2.5cm (1 in) off the end of the stems, using a long slanting cut, and then give them a long drink of water before inserting them in the foam block.

CHOOSING THE CONTAINER AND ORNAMENT

The glazed china figurine in our display is that of a 'bunny girl' sitting on a stool. In artistic terms, she is used to balance the tall vertical thrust of the main display. Admittedly, it is most unlikely that you have an identical figurine, but any china statuette, provided it is a similar size and its colours tone in with the flowers, can be used instead. If you have no figurines, a pink and white conch shell, a piece of coral, or a small candle in its holder will also make a pleasing focal point.

The flower container, a shallow plastic bowl, or 'posy bowl', as it is called in the trade, is inexpensive and a neutral colour. It doesn't matter that it has nothing attractive to offer in its own right, as it is largely hidden by the overhanging eucalyptus in the final display. If you have a shallow china dish, in white or a pastel colour, you could use this. The small rectangular tray which carries the whole display is also white plastic, but again any flat container, such as a plastic tea tray, of similar shape and size will do. If you prefer to make your arrangement more elaborate you could use a tin tea tray in a co-ordinating shade to the flowers you have chosen.

CHOOSING THE SETTING

The best position for a front-facing asymmetrical arrangement such as this is a hall table which backs into a wall. A hallway is a good place for immediate impact for visitors. Alternatively if you have the space, the arrangement can sit on a tall shelf against a wall in any room of the house that you have chosen.

Comparative Displays

An arrangement featuring just one flower variety emphasizes the essential beauty of the blooms whose subtle qualities may be lost in a mixed flower design. For example, delicate violets. The series of arrangements which follows demonstrates the impact you can make with displays using a single flower type. Three inventive arrangements with each of three flower varieties show step-by-step some of the myriad possibilities. Limiting yourself to flowers from one variety of plant material can be challenging. The interest in a display has to come from some other element than just the obvious contrast in plant materials, and this encourages you to be imaginative in your flower arranging.

EMPHASIS

One of the main reasons for choosing flowers of a single type is to focus attention solely on the flower colour. A massed-dome design does just this, and its use of compactly-packed flowerheads highlights the colour of the blooms. A massed dome display based entirely on flowers can be quite costly, done on a large scale, so it's best to keep to a smallish container, say 15-20cm (6-8 in) in diameter. To make a domed display, use a fairly shallow, straight-sided dish – a soufflé, casserole or baking dish or a short storage jar would be ideal. Fill the top of the container with a piece of crumpled wire mesh and fix it firmly in place with two lengths of florist's adhesive tape. Cut the stems of four or five flowers to the maximum height required, and place them in the centre of the dish. Cut other flowers to increasingly shorter lengths and arrange them around the first stems until those at the outside appear to be sitting on the container rim. These last flowers will hide the supporting wire.

INDIVIDUAL BEAUTY

The inverted cone or fan shape is a variation of the massed-dome design in which all but the central stems are positioned at an angle. This is a gracious and adaptable style much favoured in formal decor. Fan shaped designs look very good on a side table beside a wall, on a dining table or, in the right proportion, on a coffee table. Use any fairly shallow bowl as a container, although sloping sides which follow the direction of the stems are an advantage. Fix a large, round, heavy pinholder with a few pieces of florist's adhesive clay to the bottom of a dry bowl. Partly fill the bowl with water, cut the chosen flower stems to a single length and press the stems into the pinholder. When the arrangement is finished the stems should spread out evenly so that from whichever side the design is viewed it will look like a fan.

When inserting the flowers onto the pinholder, ensure that the stems are positioned close enough together so that the pinholder is concealed completely.

LEFT A dainty arrangement of roses is enhanced by the addition of soft sprigs of delicate maidenhair fern.

RIGHT *The rounded mass of white achillea flowerheads, arranged with variegated ivy ably demonstrates the beauty of a single flower arrangement.*

SHAPES

Traditionally, an elegant, geometric-style design such as a triangle or a crescent comprises a selection of flowers of varying shapes – some long and pointed, others full and rounded, and a few in between. However, although it is easier to achieve stylized shapes with flower types of graduated sizes and shapes, it is not essential.

If you include some flowers that are in bud and others at more advanced stages of development, you can achieve a considerable variety of shape with a single flower type. For example, use irises that are both half-opened and full-developed; or team undeveloped freesia buds with their lovely full-opened, cone-shaped flowerheads.

With the addition of a selection of foliage all shapes are possible. For example, you can create a triangle shape on a pedestal. To do this secure a piece of soaked florist's foam in a container and outline the triangle shape with slender stems of foliage. Position short leafy sprays or more substantial individual leaves close to the foam. Fill in the shape by placing buds at the points and fully-opened flowers to from the central focal point of the arrangement.

Creating a crescent or curving shape is just as simple. Outline the shape with gentle arching foliage stems or branches – slender pussy willow, broom or berberis would be appropriate – and fill in the shape with stems that are at every stage of development.

LESS RIGID DESIGNS

Some flowers, by reason of their floppy stems, such as buttercups; for their totally informal connotations such as forget-me-nots, are more suitable to a relaxed less rigid approach. Then, too, you may simply prefer informal decor, and want your flower arrangements to match. After all, a traditional triangular display of stiff lilies may be somewhat incongrous in a rambling country cottage.

In simple arrangements the relationship between the blooms and their container is the one of the central elements of the design, so choose the container with care. Minute flowers such as forget-me-nots and the even more delicate gypsophila, (baby's breath) can appear as a generous floral haze, as long as they are not overshadowed by a dominant container. A deep, straight-sided bowl in grey, mint-green or misty blue would be ideal. With stems that drape naturally, very little of the container will show, so any suitable toning colour would look attractive.

MULTIPLE POSSIBILITIES

The following arrangements will give you some ideas for single variety displays. Using the flowers, chrysanthemums, irises and tulips, which are readily available, you can duplicate these simple, but unusual arrangements.

Creative Comparisons
CHRYSANTHEMUMS

container. A further benefit of arranging with chrysanthemums is that, given proper conditioning, the display should last for up to two weeks.

The following arrangements all use chrysanthemums as the main element – the foliage used to complement the flowers is eucalyptus. One of the arrangements also requires pine cones – this adds interesting texture to a glass vessel.

LEFT A riotous profusion of golden-orange chrysanthemums, with their splendid mop-headed texture, are simply perfect for using in a variety of arrangements. You don't have to restrict yourself to late summer theme either, as the following three arrangements prove.

I f you regularly buy a bunch of inexpensive flowers on the way home, don't just drop them hastily into a vase. Instead try these quick and easy, but exceptionally stylish arrangements. All you need is a container, one or two bunches of chrysanthemums and a few sprays of foliage.

The pleasure of arranging chrysanthemums lies in their versatility. Available in a glorious array of colours, chrysanthemums suit many kinds of displays, whether used on their own, mixed with foliage or added to a mixed arrangement as a filler flower. Part of their adaptability is that chrysanthemums are suited to both traditional and modern styles, as shown in the designs that follow.

Spray chrysanthemums are most typically seen in tall vertical or triangular arrangements. However, when working with chrysanthemums you may find that short flower stems break off easily. These need not go to waste; use them for a miniature arrangement in a separate small vase or

QUICK CONDITIONING

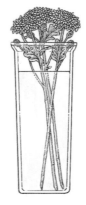

1 Cut each stem at a 45° angle and make a vertical slit about 5cm (2 in) long. Cut and slit stems under water for best results.
2 Remove the lower leaves from flower stems and plunge flowers into deep water so that roughly two

thirds of the stems are covered.
3 Add cut-flower feed in liquid or crystal form (available from florists) to the vase water before arranging the flowers.

LEFT This attractive flower container is an ordinary wicker basket painted white to contrast with the orange and green of the arrangement. Florist's foam, taped or tied to a waterproof container concealed inside the basket, provides the moisture for this traditional domed display.

1 Trim the eucalyptus stems to varying lengths and remove the lower leaves. Push the stems gently into the florist's foam and spread the foliage outwards at the sides for balance, and upwards in the centre.

2 Cut the chrysanthemum stems diagonally to different lengths leaving clusters of blooms on each stem. Remove some of the lower leaves by hand and arrange the flowers in the foam.

3 Position the tallest chrysanthemum blooms around the central eucalyptus sprays, the next tallest at the sides, and lastly place the tiniest flower blooms and buds at the front of the display.

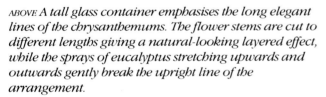

ABOVE A tall glass container emphasises the long elegant lines of the chrysanthemums. The flower stems are cut to different lengths giving a natural-looking layered effect, while the sprays of eucalyptus stretching upwards and outwards gently break the upright line of the arrangement.

1 Cut the stems of the eucalyptus sprays and the flowers, diagonally, to different lengths. Leave some of the flower stems much longer than the rest and remove leaves on the lower part of the stems.

2 Position the eucalyptus sprays in the container, with the longest stems in the centre, then add the chrysanthemums placing the tallest at the back leaning towards the handle and the smallest at the front.

3 Wash the pine cones thoroughly to remove dust and any insects and push them gently down into the water. As well as looking attractive they will help to keep the stems in place.

LEFT A wicker box makes an unusual container for this traditional low-lying display. The flowers are inserted into a foam base, taped to a hidden waterproof container and arranged in a long horizontal line to resemble jewels spilling out of a box. The lid should be propped up by a cocktail stick, to avoid crushing the blooms. When building up the display, check regularly that none of the flowers will be hidden by the lid.

1 Vary the stem lengths when cutting the eucalyptus; push the longest stems into the foam at an angle so that they drape over the sides of the box, and position the shortest sprays in the centre.

2 Cut the chrysanthemum sprays to short and long lengths and remove the lower leaves by hand. Place the shortest clusters of blooms in the front and centre and the longest at the sides.

3 Make sure that the chrysanthemums are positioned informally to cover the sides as well as the front of the box. Prop the lid gently on top, using a twig or cocktail stick.

Creative Comparisons
*W*HITE IRISES

can always ease back the flower petals. The following three displays show you how to create modern, Oriental-look and abstract displays.

As with the previous three arrangements of chrysanthemums, the flowers are the main element of the display. The additional ingredients here are all types of foliage; ming fern for the Oriental-look, ti leaves for the abstract, and bear grass for the modern display.

If you can't get ming fern, use a few sprigs from the popular house-plant, *Asparagus Sprengeri.*

LEFT White irises are the perfect flowers to use when you want to create an elegant arrangement. Their clean, crisp lines seem to lend themselves perfectly to modern, formal flower designs. With deft arranging, however, you can achieve totally different-looking results.

Tall, and timelessly classic white irises seem that little bit more special than blue irises. Explore their pure simplicity by trying out our three featured designs, using pure white irises.

When you think of irises it is usual to picture deep blue-purple flowers. White irises, however, are a fresh and more unusual alternative that add a simple sophistication to spring flower designs.

White florist's iris is available for most of the year. Each delicate flowerhead is made up of three outer petals, or falls, and three inner petals, with three yellow styles projecting in between. The flowers are carried on stems of up to 60cm (24 in) in height.

Tall and elegant, white irises look strik-

ing on their own, in the right container with just the minimum of foliage. Choose long-stemmed foliage such as bear grass or ti leaves, the line of which will complement the iris flowers. Alternatively, trailing stems of ivy from the garden contrast effectively with the clean, straight iris stems. Irises also mix well with other flowers. Combine white irises with yellow and blue varieties and red tulips to create a tall, multi-coloured display, or arrange white irises with other pure white flowers such as white lilies, roses and tulips, to make a gorgeous, radiant display perfect for a special occasion.

If your iris flowers have not fully opened in time for the special day, don't panic, you

BUYING AND CONDITIONING

● The best time to buy irises, whether blue, white or yellow, is when the buds are just beginning to show colour.

● Avoid buying irises in bud if the tips of the flower are dry, as the flowers will not open properly.

● Irises drink a lot of water and the stems tend to dry out quickly once cut, so it is advisable to re-cut the stems of the arranged flowers from time to time.

● Try to keep irises away from heat, and also fruit and vegetables, as they are sensitive to ethylene gas. If the flowers are well-conditioned they will last up to seven days in the vase.

LEFT This blue and white patterned china vase is an ideal container for long, elegant iris stems as its narrow neck provides support for the stems.

1 Fill the bottom of a tall, chinese-patterned, blue and white vase with a large hand-sized ball of scrunched-up cellophane. This will raise the base level and allow the iris stems to stand taller in the vase. Fill the vase three-quarters full with water. Cut off the stem ends of the ming fern (*Asparagus densiflorus*) and place two stems, about 40cm (16 in) long, upright in the vase.

2 Trim three white iris stems to vary their heights slightly, but leave them tall. Position them in the vase so that they stand vertical and face forward. Place one stem in the centre, one stem to the left and one stem to the right.

3 Gently open out the petals of another two irises and cut their stems fairly short, to about 15-20cm (6-8 in). Place them near the mouth of the vase, to create a strong diagonal line.

FAR LEFT *The stark elements of this abstract display aptly highlight the natural beauty of white irises.*

1 Secure a pinholder with a piece of florist's adhesive clay. Insert four large, black ti leaves into the pinholder, arrange them so that they arch; one vertical, two to the left and one to the right. Strelitzia leaves could be used as an alternative.

2 Cut four stems of half-open white iris to different lengths. The tallest flower should be about 30cm (12 in) high. The other iris stems should be progressively shorter. Position each iris so that they form a vertical line of flowers alternating left and right of an imaginary centre line. As a rough guide, the third iris stem will be about half the height of the first stem.

3 Position a further three open irises in the lower half of the display in the centre of the pinholder. Carefully pour water into the shallow tray until the pinholder is just submerged. Disguise the pinholder if wished, by covering it with a handful of pebbles.

RIGHT *This simple all-round display of irises and bear grass has a soft romantic feel. Place on casually-draped cloth to emphasize the effect.*

1 Fill a large, white urn-shaped vase two-thirds full with water. Cut off the brown stem ends of a generous bunch of bear grass, removing the bottom 5cm (2 in). Place about 40 stems of bear grass in the vase. Fan out the bear grass so that it arches naturally over the sides of the container in an even spread.

2 Cut off the white section of each iris stem, about 5cm (2 in) from the end, at a slant. Place six, half-open irises, in the centre of the vase. Arrange them in a circle formation with each flowerhead facing outwards, creating an all-round display. Keep the iris foliage on the stems.

3 Next select 10 more fully open irises and gently ease back the white petals to further open the flowerheads. Cut each successive stem about 5cm (2 in) shorter than the previous one, so that the flowers occupy different levels in the display. Place the most open blooms nearest to the rim of the vase.

Creative Comparisons
TULIPS

heavy drinkers, it is hard for them to take up enough water. Tulip stems twist and turn naturally towards the light.

The following three displays show how such traditional flowers as tulips can look stunning arranged in less conventional ways than might be expected. To achieve the different finished results with tulips, eucalyptus leaves, a piece of bleached branch, and some small pebbles have been used.

LEFT Beautiful red tulips, no longer only come from Amsterdam! Available all year round, they are always a popular choice for arrangements, bringing a splash of vibrant lightness to any room. Surprisingly versatile, tulips are perfect when something a little out-of-the-ordinary is called for.

BUYING AND CONDITIONING

Buy tulips when the buds are tightly closed but their colour is clearly showing. The upper half of the bud should be coloured while the rest of the bud is still green. Tulips showing no colour rarely open. Tulips will take about three or four days for their petals to open out fully and should then last a further week in displays.

It is important to condition tulips thoroughly before you begin arranging to get the maximum flower life. If you have bought tulips from the florist cut off the white lower end of the stem 2.5cm (1 in) and place them in deep, tepid water as soon as you get them home. Before you begin arranging, allow them a few hours to take up water. A type of cut-flower food is sold specially for tulips. Add this to the vase water to keep it clean and free of bacteria.

Available in the winter and spring months in a great variety of vivid hues, tulips are relatively inexpensive to buy. Try these beautifully simple arrangements, and follow our tips for long-lasting flowers.

Although tulips are now available in the winter months, their natural flowering time is spring. During spring the flowers are of the best quality and least expensive. There are hundreds of varieties of tulips on sale in a wide range of bright colours – red, yellow, orange, pink, purple and white – as well as the more unusual bi-coloured blooms. 'Appledoorn', a very popular variety which has single, red, goblet-shaped flowers is used in the following three arrangements.

Tulips are interesting and sometimes frustrating flowers to work with because however you decide to arrange them, they will always move in response to the light. Many florists think this makes them difficult to manage, but if you adopt a slightly less rigid style of arranging, you will achieve pleasing results. With a little imagination and confidence you can show off your tulips to their best advantage.

As with other bulb flowers, avoid using tulips in florist's foam. Use alternative forms of stem support such as chicken wire, pinholders or pebbles, or just arrange them simply in a vase. Top up the vase water frequently, since their soft stems are difficult to insert and, being very

LEFT The long elegant stems of tulips combine beautifully with pale-green scented eucalyptus sprays to create this graceful, arching fan-shaped display. No holding tricks are needed as the shape of this white china vase provides all the necessary stem support.

1 Fill a white tulip-shaped vase two-thirds full with tepid water and add cut-flower food. Arrange two long sprays of eucalyptus, cut to a length of 45cm (18 in) to the right and left of the vase. Position the eucalyptus carefully so that it arches outwards over the two lips of the vase.

2 Insert four tulips about 38cm (15 in) long, complete with their foliage, into the vase. Place them at equal distances apart in the vase. Allow their stems to overlap one another to form a criss-cross network of support in the vase. Place a fifth stem standing upright in the centre.

3 Continue adding about another eight tulips of the same height to the vase, positioning the flowers to the left or right, depending on the direction they naturally lean towards. Pack the vase with flowers and their foliage, turning the vase as you work to ensure it looks full from all angles.

LEFT This arrangement uses only a few tulips to create a strong bright impact. The tulips follow the simple curving line of a bare bleached branch which adds an Oriental look to the display.

1 Secure a pinholder to the centre of a shallow white dish with a blob of florist's adhesive clay. Fill the dish two-thirds full with tepid water and add cut-flower food. Insert a bleached branch firmly into the centre of the pinholder so that it stands up straight. Use the branch as the frame for your arrangement.

2 Cut the tulips to different lengths. Measure the tulips against the branch to determine their approximate height. Cut the three tallest stems with tighter buds so that they are about 5cm (2 in) shorter than the highest branch. Position the tall tulips into the centre of the pinholder, close to the branch. Place two slightly shorter tulips about 5cm (2 in) further down the display to create a middle level and to show off all the flowerheads. Gently ease back the outer petals on these two tulips to open up the flowerheads fully.

3 Insert another two tulips, with more open flowers, low down in the display to mask the pinholder, or use pebbles or marbles to hide the mechanics if wished.

LEFT A rectangular, clear glass vase brimming with vibrant red tulips creates a stunning array of flowers in a bed of sand and pebbles. Place this simple modern arrangement at eye level. Note how your display changes as the flowers start to open.

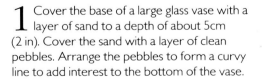

1 Cover the base of a large glass vase with a layer of sand to a depth of about 5cm (2 in). Cover the sand with a layer of clean pebbles. Arrange the pebbles to form a curvy line to add interest to the bottom of the vase.

2 The more tulips you use, the more stunning the result. Cut all the red tulips to a length of about 25cm (10 in) so that they do not stand too tall above the rim of the vase. Cut the stems at a slant and leave the foliage on the stems to bulk out the display.

3 Fill the entire vase working your way into the centre of the vase. Allow some leaves to overlap the edge of the container. The flowers will support one another so do not push the stems right into the sand. It will not be possible to precisely arrange each flowerhead as tulip stems curve towards light.

Using the Spectrum

The key to using flower colour creatively is in the simple spectrum featured below. You will see that the circle is divided into segments – and the colours are actually placed in order in which they appear in the rainbow. The way in which these colours relate to each other allows us to create widely different effects in flower designs.

PRIMARY AND SECONDARY HUES

The three primary colours, the ones you cannot make by mixing other colours together, are of course red, blue and yellow. Between them are the secondary colours which are made by mixing the two primaries on either side. Therefore, orange is between red and yellow, green between yellow and blue, and mauve between blue and red.

HARMONIZING AND CONTRASTING HUES

It is easy to remember which colour harmonize together: any colours adjacent on the colour wheel constitute harmonizing colours; these which are directly opposite each other are termed 'contrasting'.

For example, it is because yellow and green are next to each other on the colour wheel that green and yellow foliage, sharpened with bright yellow flowers, would look so harmonious. Another example is red and orange which also are adjacent colours creating harmony in a hot and spicy arrangement of summer flowers.

TINTS, TONES AND SHADES

The tints, tones and shades of any one basic colour will always look good together. Think of a brilliant crimson gerbera. Imagine that colour mixed with a little white and you might have the colour of a deep pink carnation. Add more white (on an imaginary palette) and you have a soft pastel, the colour of the palest pink tulip. Different as they may be, they are both tints (the result of adding white to a particular hue) of the colour you started with – crimson. Arrange these same flowers together in a vase and they will blend perfectly.

Any basic colour or hue mixed with grey, which gives more subtle colour, is known as a tone; mixed with black and the colour becomes a shade. Add tones and shades of a basic colour such as red and you will create a soft and subtle display.

So by referring to the spectrum and the positioning of these six basic hues, you will be able to see at a glance a whole range of options which are open to you to mix and blend in your arrangements.

WEIGHT OF TONES

The depth of colour and the way it is used have a significant effect on the appearance of an arrangement. Strong, dark, rich shades can have a heavy appearance. A pale pastel pink container used to display dark

ABOVE RIGHT A joyous medley of hues combine to create a vibrant display that brightens up any setting.

red flowers might look as if it is being squashed under the visual weight of the colours. A blend of perfectly harmonious flowers, such as lime-green tobacco plant flowers, pale green zinnias, light blue scabious and deep mauve irises, with all the darkest purple flowers at the top of the design, may appear top heavy. Placing some of the darkest flowers at the base, close to the centre of the arrangement, will add visual stability – or what some arrangers refer to as 'colour ballast'.

In any mixture of flower colours however well matched and harmonious, some of them will predominate. The way to judge is to hold up the bunch, half-close your eyes, and see which flowers seem to prevail over the others. In any group, these flowers are likely to be white, bright, sharp yellow, deep red, blue, purple, or brown. Which ones play this leading role will depend on the colour balance of the rest of the group.

These predominant flowers are the ones that need watching. If they are positioned at random throughout the design, the result is unlikely to be graceful and harmonious. This is because, at first, the eye will be drawn to these flowers. If the predominant flowers are placed with no apparent thought, the design may well look awkward and discordant.

The solution is to place these powerful colours so they make an easy, rhythmic shape; for example, a gently curving 'S' shape (the classic Hogarth curve), ranging from the top to the bottom of the arrangement, with a group of the eye-catching flowers close to the centre base.

ADVANCE AND RETIRE

Colours have the ability to deceive the eye – which is a useful trick in flower arranging. Warm colours such as red and orange make the flowers seem closer than they are, cool colours like green and blue seem further away. In a multi-coloured arrangement, try this for yourself. Place the warm colours at the front, with the cooler ones slightly recessed, and the design will appear to have an enhanced dimension.

Singular Choice

This display is quite ordinary in terms of scale and design, being a medium-sized, all-round, traditional domed shape. Its character and strength come from the huge, globe-like blooms of African marigolds: the unusual, yellow-and-green colour scheme which gives stylish monochromatic flair, and the completely unpretentious container – a terracotta flower pot.

CHOOSING THE FLOWERS

African marigolds (*Tagetes erecta* cultivars) are the most striking flowers used. These half-hardy annuals belong to the daisy, or *Compositae* family, and are Mexican, not African, in origin. They are not often sold as cut flowers, but you may be able to order some in advance; ideally, the flowers should just be starting to open.

An alternative source is garden centres which sell bedding trays, or flats, or individual pots of African marigolds, in bud or flower. Buy a tray, or flat, if necessary, and plant out the extra flowers in your garden in a bed, a border, window box or tub. Treat the plants from which you cut the flowers in the same way and they will produce more, but smaller, flowers until the plants are killed eventually by frost in late autumn.

VARIATION ON A YELLOW THEME

Though bright-orange and bright-yellow African marigolds are the most widely available varieties, they also come in pale yellow and even creamy white, but you would probably have to grow these from seed. Huge, bright-yellow chrysanthemums, zinnias or dahlias can be used instead. Yellow carnations also can be used, but they come in pastel or lemon-yellow tints, not the strong, rich yellow shown. The slightly smaller heads of French marigolds could be substituted, but you may have to scale down the display, as their stems are a lot shorter than those of African marigolds.

SOFT TEXTURES

Celosia, or Prince-of-Wales' feather, is closely related to the curiously convoluted cockscomb flowers and also to the hanging tassel flowers of love-lies-bleeding; all are tropical half-hardy annuals. In this display, the airy plumes of Prince of Wales' feather contrast with the dense, rounded forms of the African marigold. As well as yellow, there are orange and red plumed forms: dwarf forms could be used with French marigold, for a miniature version.

Prince of Wales' feather is a popular summer bedding plant, available in trays, or flats, and individual pots from garden centres. It is sometimes sold as a house plant, though this is usually more expensive and short-lived indoors. The cut flowers last longer if the stem ends are dipped briefly in boiling water, followed by a long, cold drink. Golden rod may be ued as a substitute.

GOLDEN GLOBES

The bright-yellow, globe-like craspedia flowers look like smaller versions of African marigolds, and they are also members of the daisy family, originally from New Zealand, Craspedia is more common as dried flowers than fresh, but you might be able to order some from your florist in advance. Alternatively, use the tight, ball-shaped flowerheads of achillea, tansy, cotton lavender or flat, plate-shaped yarrow flowers in as fresh a yellow as you can get it.

PREPARING THE CONTAINER

A porous terracotta pot can be made waterproof by lining it first with Cellophane or a small plastic bag, ensuring that the drainage hole in the bottom is well covered to avoid leakage.

Next, cut a block of florist's foam to fit inside the pot with 2.5cm (1 in) extending above the rim. Soak the foam in water and insert into the pot.

If there is any space between the foam and the pot, fill it with expanded clay granules, available from larger garden centres, around the florist's foam. These will anchor the foam and help it to retain moisture. Trim the Cellophane close in around the pot's rim so no overhang is visible.

As the rough terracotta pot will scratch some surfaces, use the base as a template to cut out a circle of dark felt and glue it firmly to the bottom of the pot.

MAKING A GOLDEN DISPLAY

1 Prepare the terracotta pot (see box). Insert the foliage around the collar of the pot as in a biedermeier arrangement. Remove the bottom leaves from the birch branches and cut to about 13cm (5 in). Push the stems in at an angle so they point slightly downwards. Alternate the birch leaves with stems of variegated privet leaves.

4 Next, lighten the arrangement with short green sprigs of the euphorbia. The delicate shape and the fresh green colour of these leaves gives textural contrast to the heavy yellow blooms. Don't forget to dip the stem ends in boiling water first and then give them a cool drink, or the milky latex will clog the stems and they will wilt quickly.

INGREDIENTS

1 12 large, yellow African marigolds
2 1 bunch of euphorbia
3 1 bunch of nigella seedheads
4 1 bunch of yellow celosia
5 1 bunch of craspedia
6 2 branches of beech leaves

7 young, variegated privet leaves
8 2 branches of birch foliage
9 terracotta flower pot
10 Cellophane
11 florist's foam
12 clay granules

2 Start introducing the marigolds. Place the smaller flowerheads around the edge of the arrangement, keeping them to the same length as the foliage and slanting downwards. Place the tallest marigold in the centre of the foam to set the height of the display and place five of the largest blooms around it; space them out so you can appreciate each bloom.

3 Use the green seedheads of the nigella as a filler, positioning them all over the display. Build up more of a pointed structure than a rounded one to balance with the shape of the terracotta pot. Insert the celosia in a circle to offset the green with more yellow. It is important not to put the celosia first as the thick stems may break up the foam.

Garden spurge, or euphorbia, could be listed equally well under foliage. Its flowers are tiny, but its foliage and the decorative round bracts that surround the tiny flowers are always highly valued by flower arrangers. Cut the stem ends, singe or dip briefly in boiling water, then follow with a long cool drink. Otherwise, the milky white latex clogs the stem, and they wilt.

Fresh nigella (love-in-a-mist) seedheads are a clear, bright green shortly after the blue flower petals fall. As they dry, the seedheads gradually become a duskier, greyer green, often with maroon or wine-red stripes or overtones. If you grow love-in-a-mist in your garden, you should have a ready supply of fresh seedheads: if not, order it from your florist.

CHOOSING THE FOLIAGE

Fresh beech, birch and golden-leaved and variegated privet leaves are shown and all are sold commercially. Virtually any plain green or yellow or yellow-variegated foliage could be substituted, but complicated or sophisticated foliage would be wrong for this simple display.

CHOOSING THE CONTAINER

An old-fashioned terracotta flower pot is used here.

Plastic flower pots, though often of the same terracotta colour, would not have the same appeal at all. Being lightweight, they also lack the stability of terracotta. For a similar rural effect, you could use a lined wicker basket without a handle.

CHOOSING THE SETTING

This display is a 'movable feast' and could go in virtually any room and in any position in the house – provided of course, that the room or furniture decor does not clash with the predominating yellow colour of the arrangement.

Remember that terracotta pots are rough clay and if they have been used for potted plants, they may be dirty with a build-up of white salts from plant fertilizers, or of algae or moss. You can wash and scrub them clean, but wipe the base dry. As a further precautionary measure protect furniture from scratches with a small plate or mat positioned underneath the pot.

5 Add a few sprigs of beech leaves. This bold, distinctively shaped foliage will give variety to the display. By contributing a darker shade of green, they will aid in highlighting the brilliant yellow of the marigolds. Turn the display slowly and fill in any gaps; check that the colours of the flowers and foliage are all well balanced.

6 Finally, to add to the assortment of shapes and textures, carefully position the craspedia. Place them at random and standing quite far out in the display. If they had been included at an earlier stage, they would have been lost. The final result is a bright, saturated yellow all-round arrangement to brighten up your kitchen table or bathroom.

Harmonious Hues

This arrangement of pink, mauve and blue flowers is based on using harmonious colours together to create a subtle haze that is pleasing to the eye. In this display no one single colour or flower stands out more than another.

CHOOSING THE FLOWERS

Two shapes dominate the display: the huge, round heads of hydrangea, repeated in the smaller heads of chincherinchee, and the spiky flowerheads of statice and liatris. There are many possible alternatives, but for consistency, use these two basic shapes.

Few flowers are as large and round as hydrangeas but they are the ideal shape, and shrubs have abundant blooms. If you don't grow hydrangeas, your florist can supply them, but you may have to order them in advance.

Before arranging hydrangeas, sear the cut ends with a flame, or dip them briefly in boiling water, then follow with a long drink. Better still, submerge the entire head and stem in cool water for several hours.

Instead of hydrangeas, you could use the rounded flowerheads of the snowball tree, *Viburnum opulus* 'Sterile'. The enormous lilac-flowered ornamental allium, *Allium giganteum* also would be suitable, and some dahlias and large-flowered chrysanthemums can equal a hydrangea head in bulk. Unfortunately, neither allium or viburnum come in blue, although you can get pink and mauve varieties. As a last resort, use dried hydrangeas, but avoid getting their stems wet or they will rot quickly.

Liatris, also known as gayfeather, is unusual in that it opens from the top of the flower spike down, rather than from the bottom up. Buy liatris when only the top blooms have opened. It is a North American member of the daisy family, and makes a striking perennial for sunny, sheltered gardens and well-drained soil. The varieties range from 60-180cm (2-6 ft) in height.

Liatris can be a difficult flower to use successfully in arrangements because of its unusual shape. It can look striking with just foliage in modern arrangements, but it also combines comfortably with rounded blooms, such as hydrangea, as can be seen in the featured display.

There are white forms of liatris, and the deep-blue 'August Glory', as well as the pinky-mauve variety used in the featured display. Liatris is grown commercially for cutting all year round, but you may have to order it in advance from the florist. Otherwise, use small-flowered gladioli in shades of lilac or pink, or flower spikes of herbaceous veronica or speedwell from the garden.

SELECTING SMALLER FLOWERS

Statice is better known in its dried form

Adjacent tones on the spectrum, in this case, yellow, orange and red, combine in a scheme with overall harmony. The different flower shapes, from flat to open trumpets, make a dramatic outline.

rather than fresh, but the fresh flower is slightly more colourful. You may have to buy mixed-colour bunches of statice; if so, hang the unused flowers upside-down to dry. Alternatively, use fresh perennial statice. Although most are white, some have a definite lavender tint to them, and are worth looking out for. You also could use freshly dried, blue annual statice, but avoid old stems which may be dusty.

Brodiaea has delicate, trumpet-shaped blue flowers and graceful, leafless stems. A North American member of the amaryllis family, brodiaea can be grown in sunny, sheltered gardens or in greenhouses in cooler districts. It's grown commercially for the cut-flower trade but, again, order it in advance from your florist.

Chincherinchees are South African bulbous plants and very popular at Christmas, but available all year round. Buy them when one or two flowers are open, and about a third of the buds are showing colour. Avoid blooms with yellow stems, as this is a sure indication that the flowers are past their best. If you can't find chincherinchees, use long-stemmed, white, double freesias.

Eucalpytus is always referred to as 'blue' – it's even sometimes referred to as 'blue gum' – but seen in contrast to the deep-blue of vase and other flowers, eucalyptus foliage takes on a definite grey tinge. You could use leather leaf fern, blue-grey rue or the grey foliage of *Senecio Greyi* 'Sunshine' in place of eucalyptus.

CHOOSING THE CONTAINER

A marbled glass vase with a classical shape and narrow, high neck is used for this display. It's unlikely that you'll be able to get an identical one, but try to choose a vase with distinctive colours. A solid blue, mauve or pink vase is fine, but it's more interesting to choose one with a marbled, speckled or other textural or painted effect, with one main colour enriched

CREATING A FRESH-FLOWER DISPLAY

1 Fill the vase two-thirds full with water. Add cut-flower food to the vase water. Remove the lower leaves from six stems of purple and mauve statice. Cut the stems at a slant and to twice the height of the vase. Place them vertically in the centre of the vase. No foundation is necessary – the stems will support each other. The statice sets the basic silhouette of the display.

4 Strip away the papery brown sepals from around the flowers on eight stems of chincherinchee. Cut the chincherinchee stems at equal lengths but leave the stems long enough to come well above the height of the hydrangeas. Place them at even intervals around the display. The small, white flowers provide highlights that stand out against the other, deeply coloured flowers.

INGREDIENTS

1 6 stems of purple and mauve statice
2 8 stems of blue brodiaea
3 3 stems of eucalyptus
4 5 stems of pink and blue hydrangeas
5 8 stems of pink-mauve liatris
6 8 stems of chincherinchee
7 opaque glass vase
8 floristry knife

2 Strip the lower leaves from five open hydrangea heads. Choose blooms in mixed shades to co-ordinate perfectly with the colours on the vase. Cut four of the stems to even lengths and place them around the rim of the vase. Make sure that there is plenty of space between each flowerhead. Leave one hydrangea stem longer than the others and place it to one side of the vase.

3 Cut three woody eucalyptus stems at a slant, each one the same length. Place each stem, at an even distance apart, around the mouth of the vase. Position them so that the stem ends are in water, but the leafy stems trail over the rim of the vase. Eucalyptus is a good choice of foliage as the blue-grey leaves link with the blue flowers and also with the decorative finish of the vase.

5 Cut eight stems of purple liatris twice the height of the vase. Strip away the lower leaves. Insert them vertically in the centre of the display and allow them to settle into gentle angles, radiating out from the centre. The spiky liatris stems contrast effectively with the rounded hydrangea heads and the soft mauve shades provide another colour link between the flowers and the vase.

6 Strip away the lower, papery sepals from eight stems of blue brodiaea as you did for the chincherinchee. Cut the stems to graduated heights. Group them in the middle of the display to make a rounded fan shape of brodiaea stems within the other flowers. The strong blue colouring of the brodiaea flowers links up with the blue veining on the vase and the purple-blue shades of the other flowers.

with subtle swirls of other complementary colours.

You might be able to find a container of a suitable size and shape but an uninspiring colour in a junk shop or at a boot sale, or you might even have one tucked away at the back of a cupboard. If so you can add to the sense of creative fulfillment and paint it to harmonize with your choice of flowers. Paint the vase with a single colour, allow it to dry, then spatter it with environment-friendly spray paint in a second, and even a third toning shade.

It is also important that the vase has a simple shape, as an intricate one would compete for attention with the flowers. Choose a vase with a narrow neck to support the flower stems. If you want to use a wide-necked container, place crumpled chicken wire or a soaked florist's foam block inside its mouth to provide sufficient support for the flowers with heavy blooms.

CHOOSING THE SETTING
The tall narrow shape of this arrangement is a bonus. Display it in pride of place on a hallway table, perhaps in front of a mirror for all-round interest. Alternatively, use the strong colours and contrasting shapes of this arrangement to bring a splash of vibrant colour to an empty summer fireplace.

Use the featured arrangement as the focal point of a grouped display. Combine it with two or three smaller vases in matching shades of pink or blue. Use at least one identical flower in each and link the colours in all for a co-ordinated appearance. Display the collection along the mantelpiece or on staggered shelves in the sitting room.

LOOKING AFTER THE DISPLAY
All the material is long lasting and, with proper care, you should be able to enjoy them for at least two weeks. Change the water regularly as the liatris pollutes it rapidly. Spray mist the flowers if they are displayed in a warm place. When they have faded, cut off the wet portion of the hydrangea, liatris, statice and eucalyptus stems and hang them, according to type, upside-down in a warm, well-ventilated place to dry out for future use.

Contrasting Flowers

POWERFUL PINKS, MAUVES AND BLUES COMBINE IN THIS DISPLAY OF HYDRANGEAS, LIATRIS,
BRODIAEA AND ANNUAL STATICE, WITH CHINCHERINCHEE AND EUCALYPTUS PROVIDING CONTRAST

The display here demonstrates how effective the use of flowers that come from opposing sides of the spectrum can be. The colours are complementary, they work well together – a floral example of opposites attracting. This arrangement boasts bold splashes of colour to give any room a visual lift, and it's eye-catching enough to feature at a special party occasion.

CHOOSING THE FLOWERS

The colours of the chosen flowers are intense – the bright-pink gerberas and deep-yellow ranunculus – for a jazzy modern look. However, if you prefer softer colours, you can tone down the shades and achieve an equally beautiful result. White hydrangeas, white gerberas and creamy-white ranunculus, for example, would give a cool, sophisticated green-and-white display; or you could use pink hydrangeas, pink gerberas and pink ranunculus for a softly feminine scheme.

Mauve-blue, lace-cap hydrangeas, with their dark-green leaves, form the bulk of the display. Mop-head hydrangeas, or the pyramid-shaped flowers of *H. paniculata*, could be substituted. If you cut your own from the garden, choose ones that have been open for a few days; immature hydrangeas are hard to condition and so their vase life will be short. If you grow oak-leaved hydrangea (*H. quercifolia*), its panicles of white flowers and oak-shaped leaves would make an unusual feature. As a bonus, the leaves turn brilliant crimson, purple or orange in autumn.

Some summer-flowering viburnums have hydrangea-like, lace-cap flowers along the length of their branches. *Viburnum plicatum tomentosum* 'Mariesii', 'Lanarth', 'Pink Beauty' or 'Rowallane' are worth growing for their beauty in the garden as well as for cut material indoors. As viburnum leaves are slightly smaller, you may want to include a few more branches just for foliage. Condition them as for hydrangeas (see box).

ALTERNATIVE SHADES

Pink gerberas are used in the featured display, but they come in many other tints. Most local florists only stock one or two colours at a time; if you want a particular colour, order it in advance to avoid disappointment. When you get the flowers home, re-cut the stems, dip them briefly in boiling water and then stand them in a deep container of water for several hours.

Gerbera flowers are the same shape as single chrysanthemums, but gerbera stems are curved, while those of chrysanthemums are poker-straight. As curving gerbera stems are a prominent feature in this display, if you can't get them, try to choose a flower of roughly the same size with a similar stem, such as anemone or tulip.

ELEGANT ARUM LILIES

A trio of white arum lilies, also known as zantedeschias, add simple elegance and strong bold lines to the arrangement. You'll almost certainly have to order arum lilies in advance. Arum lilies are grown commercially for cutting, and they have a special quality not found in other flowers of the Araceae family. Re-cut the stems when you get them home, then place the flowers up to their necks in a deep container of water and leave for several hours.

Three bright-yellow Turk's cap ranunculus make a stunning focal point; like

CONDITIONING HYDRANGEAS

Hydrangea flowers will last longer in the vase if water can be drawn up the stems easily. This won't happen if they are exposed to the air for any length of time, the stem end begins to heal over and is sealed gradually by a protective callus. This prevents water from entering the stem, thus causing the flower to starve and wilt prematurely.

Remove the seal by plunging the stem end in a few inches of boiling water. This kills those cells immersed in the water and prevents them from becoming a callus. Protect the flowerhead from the heat of the steam by covering it with a cloth or bag. The flowers absorb water through their petals, so submerging the whole head and stem under water for a few hours, after sealing the stem end also helps. Leave the stems to cool in a deep container of water before arranging.

SIX EASY STEPS TO A CONTRASTING FLOWER DISPLAY

1 Fill the vase two-thirds full with water. Following the curves of the vase across the top, divide it into four sections with criss-cross strips of clear sticky-tape. Cut the tape to length so that the ends are not visible over the edge. By dividing the vase into sections with tape, the flowers won't fall outwards to the edge of the vase.

4 Snip the ends of four bright-pink gerbera stems, keeping as much as possible of their length. In contrast with the vertical stems stems of the arum lily, the gerbera stems bend and twist, echoing the curving lines of the vase. Place all four flowers in one section at the side of the vase. Rest the flowers against each other.

INGREDIENTS
1 3 stems of hydrangea foliage
2 3 blue hydrangea flowers
3 3 stems of arum lily
4 4 stems of pink gerbera

5 3 stems of yellow ranunculus
6 vase
7 scissors
8 sticky tape

2 Begin with a dramatic grouping of hydrangea leaves. Cut the ends of three stems of hydrangea foliage that have small, under-developed flowers or none at all. Cut the stems to twice the height of the vase. Place the stems in the two middle sections so they lean on the sticky tape.

3 Cut the stems of three arum lilies at a slant in graduated lengths, the tallest one at least one flowerhead higher than the other two blooms. Place them against the back edge of the vase in a trio, with their stems standing completely straight. Position the flowerheads so that they all face in the same direction.

5 Cut three leafy hydrangea stems to the same height as the other flowers. Group them in a taped-off section on the opposite side of the vase to the pink gerberas. Place two flowerheads leaning out sideways from the display and one flower more centrally, facing forwards. Frame each flowerhead with a mass of foliage.

6 Finish with a splash of bright yellow ranunculus. Leave the stems at their full length, only re-cutting the ends at a slant. Place three flowers in a taped section in the central focal point to make a yellow group at the front of the display. Support the flowers with more hydrangea foliage if necessary. Intersperse with remaining ranunculus buds.

gerberas, they come in a wide range of bright and subtle colours. Recut the stems when you get them home, then place in a deep container of water for several hours, or overnight, before arranging.

CHOOSING THE CONTAINER

We have used a modern, white glazed china vase, roughly triangular in plan and about 20cm (8 in) across. The sides are angled outwards slightly, and the free-form, curving base creates an attractive, undulating effect. You may not be able to find an exact replica, but any tall, straight-sided or outward-angled container can be used instead, provided it has a reasonably wide neck. As well as white, you could use china glazed in a single bright colour, perhaps repeating one of the flower colours, or a modern glass cube or cylinder vase. If you use a glass container, pay special attention to the appearance of the stems and remove all of the leaves that will fall below the water-line.

The main challenge of a wide-necked container, such as the one shown, is to keep stems upright. Florist's foam and crumpled chicken wire are traditional supports, but here, clear sticky tape is criss-crossed over the rim, forming an almost invisible webbing to hold the stems in place. It's perfect for a glass container as nothing shows, or for a delicate or valuable container which could be damaged by chicken wire.

CHOOSING THE SETTING

A bright splash of flower colour will bring any indoor setting to life. The display is featured here in a modern living room against a neutral background which makes a perfect foil for the richly coloured blooms. A plain white wall would put even greater emphasis on the colour of the flowers. Even the most delicate interior colour scheme often has tiny sparks of bright colour, such as the centre of flowers on a miniature-print wallpaper or fabric. Rather than looking out of place, a brightly coloured arrangement would pick up these flecks of colour and complement the decor.

The display is front facing, so it can stand against a wall, or on a wide shelf.

Vivid Display

MAKE AN IMPACT WITH DRAMATIC SUNFLOWERS AND LATE-SUMMER BLOOMS
COMBINED IN A STRIKING VASE FOR A TRULY SPECTACULAR DISPLAY

This arresting arrangement presents the opportunity to experiment with brilliant colour combinations on a scale that would prove prohibitively expensive if other plant materials were used. By ignoring conventional colour guidelines and using colours together that some would say clash, the display defines its own frame of reference and unique character.

A special feature of the display is the ceramic vase, hand-painted with primary red, yellow and blue abstract shapes. It sets the tone of the finished design and determines the choice of flowers: bright, bold and uninhibited.

CHOOSING THE FLOWERS

All the flowers shown should be available from your florist, although you may have to order some, such as the sunflowers, in advance. If you have a garden, you can make your own substitutions.

For a long-lasting display, condition your flowers before use. Remove all the leaves that will fall below the waterline in the vase, re-cut the stems diagonally, then plunge them immediately into a bucket of water. Leave them for several hours or overnight to receive the full benefit of this treatment.

The most eye-catching flowers are the huge annual sunflowers. These North American giants can grow 3m (10 ft) high and the daisy-like flowers have a diameter of up to 25cm (10 in). A single variety has been used for this display, but occasionally double-headed stems are available. A more subdued alternative would be to use purple artichoke flowerheads.

Rudbeckias, or coneflowers, are annual or perennial members of the *Compositae* family. Their orange and yellow colour reflects the colour of the sunflowers, and the dainty flowers provide contrast in size and form. You could use coreopsis, heleniums, ligularias, pot marigolds or blanket flower (gaillardia) instead. The perennial purple coneflower (*Echinacea purpurea*) would be perfect to complement purple artichoke heads.

Fresh green amaranthus, or love-lies-bleeding, adds an elegant weeping line to the display. The stems are cut short and inserted around the rim of the container, so their drooping heads visually break up the line of the rim, and curl attractively onto the table surface. Crimson amaranthus is more common and would be just as effective. If amaranthus is not available, try using millet seedheads.

CONTRASTING SIZE AND FORM

Hot-pink nerines, or Guernsey lilies, are late-summer flowers, although they are available for an extended period from florists. In this display, the tall, leafless stems and spidery flowerheads are grouped to form a crown behind the sunflowers. Agapanthus, alstroemeria or ornamental alliums could be substituted.

The pink of the nerines is echoed in the annual China asters, or callistephus; they also come in pale blue and purple. Often, China asters are sold on relatively short stems; if you want to use the long-stemmed versions shown, mention this when you place your order. Asters or Michaelmas daisies would also be appropriate.

White flower spikes of herbaceous perennial veronica add depth to the composition and interest to the silhouette. Long-stemmed flower sprigs of shrubby veronica, or hebe, could be used, in pink, mauve, purple or white.

LACY FLOWERS

Ammi majus adds laciness to the design, in direct contrast to the dominant visual weight of the sunflowers. Bright, yellow-green fennel or dill could be used instead.

Dark-red single carnations are bunched together to one side of the arrangement,

USING CHICKEN WIRE

To secure bulky stems in place in a large arrangement that incorporates heavy-headed blooms, use crumpled chicken wire in preference to fresh florist's foam – the foam may break up with the weight of the plant material.

Using wire cutters, cut a square piece of large-meshed chicken wire, at least the height of your chosen container. Carefully bend under the edges of the wire to achieve a loose, rounded shape that will fit snugly into the neck of the vase. Place the crumpled wire into the vase and gently ease it up into a dome shape that fills the mouth of the vase completely.

ASSEMBLING YOUR VIVID DISPLAY

1 Place the crumpled chicken wire inside the neck of the vase (see box for details). Fill the vase two-thirds full of water. Remove the lower leaves from four sunflowers and trim the stems to graduated lengths. Position the sunflowers centrally. Cut the ends of four loves-lies-bleeding stems and place them around the rim of the vase.

4 Trim a medium-sized spray of forsythia foliage to 60cm (24 in). Gently bend the stem to exaggerate its natural curve. Introduce into the left-hand side of the design. Separate a bunch of gypsophila into sprigs. Place any large sprigs to the right-hand side, angled downwards to balance the forsythia foliage. Add the smaller sprigs.

INGREDIENTS
1 4 sunflowers
2 3 China asters
3 1 bunch of dyed-blue gypsophila
4 2 stems of Ammi majus
5 1 medium-sized spray of forsythia
6 5 single carnations
7 4 stems of veronica

8 3 stems of rudbeckia
9 4 stems of euonymus foliage
10 6 stems of nerine
11 4 stems of love-lies-bleeding
12 1 large spray of red beech foliage
13 brightly coloured vase
14 60cm × 60cm (2 ft × 2 ft) of chicken wire

2 Trim two stems of *Ammi majus* so that they stand about 5cm (2 in) taller than the sunflowers. This will help prevent the sunflowers overpowering the other plant material. Place the *Ammi majus* to the back left-hand side of the display. Divide a large spray of beech into three sprigs and position these around the base of the arrangement.

3 Cut the ends of three China aster stems to graduated lengths, the shortest being 30cm (12 in) high, the tallest almost the same height as the sunflowers. Position to the left-hand side of the arrangement. Balance these with three trimmed rudbeckia stems, cut to similar graduated lengths. Place the rudbeckia to the right-hand side of the display.

5 Cut four stems of veronica to graduated heights so that the tallest is a little higher than the sunflowers and the shortest stands about 45cm (18 in) tall. Position the tallest stems at the back of the other plant material and the shorter ones in the middle and to either side. The spiky veronica flowers add stark white highlights and textural contrast.

6 Cut four stems of euonymus foliage and insert two at the front of the vase and two at the back. Trim five carnation stems and group them to the left-hand side of the display. Trim the ends of five nerines, keeping as much length as possible. Add in a fan shape to the back of the vase. Position one shorter stem in the middle of the other flowers.

echoing the dark-red circles painted on the vase. You could use spray carnations instead, in red, pink or white.

Blue-dyed gypsophila looks unnatural, but is appropriate for this design as it adds colour and holds its own against the other bright colours better than if it were its usual, delicate white. If you cannot obtain ready-dyed gypsophila, place untreated stems in water to which you have added several drops of food colouring; within two hours, the gypsophila will absorb the colour.

CHOOSING THE FOLIAGE
Continuing the colourful theme, purple beech, yellow-and-green variegated euonymus and plain-green forsythia foliage are included. Purple-leaved cherry or plum could be substituted for the beech, and variegated elaeagnus for the euonymus. Almost any strong-stemmed green foliage is suitable, or yellow-leaved flowering currant or yellow-leaved mock orange.

The container is wide necked, about 15cm (6 in) across, to accommodate the many thick stems, and 30cm (12 in) high. You could paint your own unglazed ceramic vase using china paints, dabbed on with a sponge for broad areas of colour, and with a brush for more detailed straight lines.

The display should look fresh for at least four days, after which the veronica and rudbeckia will start to wilt. Remove the flowers as they fade and replace with fresh flowers and foliage. When you eventually dismantle the design it is well worth keeping some of the more exotic blooms, hang up anything that looks reasonable to air-dry. It will dry more effectively if you begin by first cutting off the lower stems. It should be possible to air-dry the gypsophila, amaranthus, coneflower and sunflower. You can then use these materials again to create another stunning arrangement, only this time it will be a dried display.

CHOOSING THE SETTING
This vivid arrangement is large and spectacular enough to appear commanding in any room in the house, whatever the decor, so the ideal setting for it, is where it can make the most impact.

CHAPTER THREE

*I*NNOVATIVE IDEAS

Truly creative flower arranging involves using much more than just flowers and today, even traditional florists are 'branching out' to include exciting, non-floral plant material in their displays. Adding the odd sprig of florist's fern to a mixed bunch of flowers has given way to a whole new approach: including a gener-ous proportion of unusual foliage in an arrangement, or even excluding flowers entirely, and creating dramatic impact with foliage alone.

There are many advantages. If you have a garden, the foliage is free, and your flower-arranging budget can stretch that much further. Using garden foliage, or even sprigs of house-plant foliage, instantly personalizes a display, and gives character to florist's flowers, such as carnations and chrysanthemums, whose own foliage is dull or non-existent. This approach also forces you to study and appreciate form and texture, and not dismiss foliage as a single, boring shade of green. You'll soon learn that foliage ranges from icy white, silver and cream through yellow, orange, red, blue and violet – all the colours of the spectrum, plus subtle, rich and smoky hues. Even similar-colour leaves can differ dramatically: the deeply furrowed, blue-grey leaves of *Hosta sieboldiana* have one effect: the lacy, delicate, blue-grey leaves of

LEFT A country-garden composition of borage flowers, marjoram, dill heads, spires of sage, angelica heads, curry plant shoots and orange calendulas.

rue, an entirely different one.

Including leafless branches from the garden in flower arrangements is equally refreshing, providing linear contrast to the mass of flowers and foliage, and instant, inexpensive height. The elegant tracery of bare contorted willow, hazel or birch branches; cone-laden larch or alder branches; spiky manzanita; or sun-bleached, scultpural ivy roots always add character and a sense of movement. Red-, yellow- or purple-barked willow or dogwood can provide all the colour a display needs, especially in winter. Even if you don't have a garden, most florists now sell a wide range of foliage and branches, and will take orders for special requests, given advance warning.

The kitchen is a fruitful source of raw material, literally! Use fresh fruit, vegetables, nuts and herbs with flowers to create a seasonal display or, by using unusual tropical fruit and vegetables, an exotic one. Hollowed-out vegetables and fruits, such as marrows or melons, can act as vases; on a smaller scale, green pepper halves or scooped-out apples can hold tiny arrangements. Wiring together chilli peppers or adding false stems to cherry tomatoes, pearl onions or mushrooms transforms them into 'fantasy flowers', ideal for creating the *piece de resistance* centrepiece of a buffet table.

The projects in this chapter show you exactly how to create all-foliage and 'mixed media' displays, but once you begin, you'll want to experiment, and make your own original arrangements. Don't be afraid to be extravagant; you can sometimes even eat the fruit and vegetables afterwards, and hang the herbs upside down to dry, getting double value for money!

ABOVE RIGHT A twirl of ivy and variegated holly forming a protective collar around the base and handle of a grey wicker basket sets off a bright display of several varieties of exotic fruit.

BELOW RIGHT It takes just a handful of mixed foliage – apple, crab apple, mulberry and periwinkle leaves to create a stylish design in an attractive, chestnut-patterned teapot.

Foliage Display

This display shows that all-foliage designs can be just as interesting and can make a refreshing change from traditional flower designs.

So capitalize on the rich variety of foliage available to flower-arrangers and create a new look.

Some of the materials used are better known as house plants than florists' foliage. House plants that have grown too big or that are spindly as a result of low winter light levels are usually pruned in spring and this is the perfect time to make this display. By removing the fresh growth at the top of a long, bare stem, you will be gaining useful arranging materials for free while encouraging the plant to bush out at the same time.

If you don't have the house plants shown, there are plenty of other house plants, garden plants and florists' foliage that can be used instead. The source of the foliage doesn't matter; what is important is the range of shapes, sizes, colour and habits of growth.

CHOOSING THE FOLIAGE
Ivy is the most versatile of the ingredients in this display: it is found in the wild, in the garden and home, and as florists' cut foliage. A green-and-white cultivar is shown, but any small-leaved ivy is suitable. If possible, try to avoid stems with soft growth at the tips, since these young leaves wilt almost as soon as they are cut. If you have no alternative, snip off the soft growth before inserting the stems into the vase.

ASPARAGUS FERN
Asparagus fern refers to a group of plants rather than one species. They are actually members of the lily family and, when mature, produce tiny white flowers and red berries – something which real ferns never do. *Asparagus densiflorus* 'Sprengeri', or emerald feather, is used here, and although more common as a house plant, it is available occasionally as florists' foliage. In addition you could use the foxtail fern, *A. densiflorus* 'Meyerii'; the sickle-thorn, *A. falcatus*; or the florists' asparagus fern, *A. plumosus*. Florists' asparagus fern is sometimes called lace fern or bridal fern because of its frequent inclusion in bridal bouquets.

Bear grass is only available from the florist, but a few leaves of cymbidium, the popular house-plant orchid, could be substituted. Another possible alternative plant is broom. Although this has small flowers, the overall effect is still green and linear and therefore very similar to bear grass.

REMOVING THORNS

Asparagus densiflorus 'Sprengeri' has small, especially vicious thorns so guard against injury before you arrange the asparagus stems. Carefully hold the asparagus fern by its fronds and snip off the green-brown thorns from the stem.

Laurustinus (*Viburnum tinus*) plays a modest, but necessary, role, adding bulk and depth to the display. One especially attractive variegated form has yellow leaf markings. Laurustinus is available as florists' foliage, but you may have to order it in advance. For a similar effect use elaeagnus, camellia or densely packed smilax.

Eucalyptus is a popular, year-round florists' foliage and *Eucalyptus gunnii*, blue gum, is perfect as a garden source of foliage for arrangements. It is hardy enough to be grown in sunny, sheltered gardens and, if cut back annually or 'stooled', can be trained to a compact shape with easy-to-reach branches.

CONIFER FOLIAGE
The conifer foliage used is from the Norfolk Island pine, *Araucaria heterophylla*, also known as house pine, Christmas-tree plant and Australian pine. It is a slow-growing house plant, related to the monkey-puzzle tree, and its branches grow in attractive, horizontal tiers. Spruce or fir from the garden or florist can be used instead.

Croton (*Codiaeum variegatum* 'Pictum') foliage is the most colourful and unusual ingredient included in this arrangement. A tropical house plant from Malaya, croton is a member of the Euphorbia family. Croton exudes a milky latex when cut which can irritate the skin. Always handle cut croton stems with care, and wash your hands immediately if latex gets on your skin. To halt the flow of latex, dip cut ends in water or powdered charcoal.

There are many different varieties of croton, with leaves which range from broadly oval to long and narrow and with yellow, scarlet, crimson, pink, orange,

HOW TO MAKE YOUR ALL-FOLIAGE DISPLAY

1 Fill a vase three-quarters full of water and add cut-flower food. Using secateurs or wire cutters, trim a length of chicken wire 60cm (24 in) long. Bend the top 2.5cm (1 in) of the chicken wire cylinder inwards to hold the flower stems in place. Insert the shaped wire into the vase so that it lies below the rim.

4 Gently bend three sprays of laurustinus to exaggerate their natural curve. Position these with the other trailing material over the rim of the vase. The white flowers add contrast to the display. Remove the lower leaves from the croton plant stem and place it as a colourful focal point in the middle of the display.

INGREDIENTS

1 *5 stems of variegated ivy*
2 *5 stems of* Asparagus densiflorus *'Sprengeri'*
3 *small bunch of bear grass*
4 *3 stems of laurustinus*
5 *3 stems of eucalyptus*
6 *1 large croton plant stem*
7 *1 large stem of Norfolk Island pine*
8 *secateurs*
9 *60cm (24 in) length of chicken wire*
10 *vase*

2 Remove any *Asparagus densiflorus* 'Sprengeri' foliage that will come below the water-line to prevent discoloration of the water. Snip off the sharp thorns from the stems (see box). Use the asparagus stems to edge the rim of the vase so that they arch naturally and give the display width.

3 Remove the lower foliage from three stems of eucalyptus and put any short sprigs you have taken off to one side for use in smaller displays. Cut the eucalyptus stems so that they stand about two and a half times the height of the vase and use them to set the height of the arrangement. Trail five stems of variegated ivy over the rim of the vase.

green, white and nearly black variegations. A large, broad-leaved form is used here to give the effect of a huge, tropical bloom. You could use a narrow-leaved form, but then you need to increase the 'filler foliage' accordingly. A largely green form would lose most of its impact.

If you keep a croton house plant in warm, humid, bright conditions, it will grow quite large, and therefore will benefit from spring pruning. Move leafless, spindly crotons to a brighter spot after cutting the top leaves off; new growth will soon appear. Cut croton foliage is sometimes available from florist shops, or you can try substituting colourful, large-leaved begonia, coleus or maranta house-plant foliage; or aucuba leaves from the garden, provided they have plenty of yellow markings.

CHOOSING THE CONTAINER

A simple, pink-beige and grey-green vase, 30cm (12 in) high, is used for this design. Any similar container would do; one that is pearlised would be especially attractive. Particularly popular during the 1950s, pearlised ceramics can be found in some antique shops. In addition, large gift shops and Oriental shops sell inexpensive, modern pearlised ceramic vases.

Another possibility would be a rough stoneware container, which you may be able to buy cheaply in a junk shop. A vase of this type, whilst following the gently rounded shape of the one shown here, could give quite a different but equally attractive 'feel' to the design, displaying foliage against a texture and colour similar to that of rockery stones or paving stones.

If a junk-shop container was slightly damaged, this would not matter, since the cascade of leaves completely covers the rim, always the most vulnerable part.

5 Divide a large branch of Norfolk Island pine into smaller sprigs. Intersperse these between the croton leaves so that you break up the massed look of the plant and prevent the colourful croton from dominating the display. Place some of the Norfolk island pine stems around the back of the arrangement to fill in any gaps.

6 Cut off the white section at the end of the bear grass to help it take up water. Divide the bear grass into small groups of about eight stems and carefully arch these in your hand. Avoid running your hand along the sharp under-side of the grass. Place the bear grass throughout the display to add a light, airy touch.

CARING FOR THE DISPLAY

Position the arrangement in a cool place, preferably out of draughts. Spray the plant material with water daily, especially the asparagus fern, and re-cut fern stems frequently to help prevent needle drop. As the foliage wilts, remove and replace with fresh material to prolong the life of the display.

Foliage Ideas

Colourful and textured foliage has all the beauty of flowers and is as versatile displayed on its own or mixed with other material. Myriad new arranging opportunities open up when you first begin to look at leaves as more than mere accessories to flamboyant flower displays.

Whether you choose to simply arrange a vase of golden leaves to filter light through a window; make a cool display of glossy and variegated foliage in a glass container or construct a more permanent and elaborate arrangement using growing houseplants – in each of these examples, foliage is sure to make an impact.

FOLIAGE WITH FLOWERS
Floral arrangements of every kind are enhanced by foliage. Foliage is a natural partner to any collection of flowers and plant materials, whether fresh or dried, formal or informal. Few designs look complete without a ruffle of leaves to balance the display base and lines of foliage interspersed between the flowers to emphasise the colours and textures.

Shining branches of glycerined leaves make the perfect outline for a large, pedestal display and a contrasting background for pretty flowers. A small bunch of old-fashioned pinks, nasturtiums and cornflowers looks more attractive if mingled with cottage-garden sprays of purple sage and santolina. A traditional domed Biedermier would look unfinished without its traditional collar of leaves, perhaps aspara-

gus fern, leather leaf fern or even ferns from the garden if you have them.

JUST FOLIAGE
Leaves have so much to offer that they can replace flowers in every style of arrangement. Carefully selected leaves span a colour range from deep purple to brilliant scarlet; vibrant orange and sharp yellow to vivid lime; fresh green and deep holly green to soft, subtle tints of grey; and silver to almost white. Shapes range from long, sword-shaped leaves, such as gladiolus and iris, to tiny rounded berberis leaves carried on long, woody stems and narrow rosemary leaves.

The design possibilities expand even more when textural differences are considered. Glossy magnolia and laurel leaves reflect light like a mirror, and sun or artificial light bounce back to illuminate a design. Mahonia and rose foliage is semi-reflective, halfway between plants with glossy leaves and those with matt leaves. The latter type includes sage, lamium, and some of the mint family. Some leaves have a deep, downy texture like velvet – silver-grey ballota and lamb's tongue (*Stachys lanata*) are particularly soft and furry.

An earthenware jar of golden ash-leaf maple or horse chestnut is a lovely way to introduce autumnal colour into the home and looks spectacular placed where the sunlight can shine through the leaves.

The leaves of a deciduous tree will eventually drop and you could throw them away. Alternatively, display a handful of colourful branches without water in a large container, such as a goldfish bowl or a heavy, rectangular glass vase. As the leaves drop, put them into the container. As the number of leaves remaining on the branches decreases and the pile in the vase increases, the emphasis of the design changes. Eventually, you will be left with a dramatic silhouette of bare stems standing in a crock of gold.

WIRING LEAVES

Wire large, colourful leaves and attach them to bare stems for a long-lasting, natural display. Cluster two to three leaves together to create a strong visual impact and conceal the fixings. Wired leaves make good companions to both fresh and dried flower arrangements.

Mount large and medium-sized leaves such as maple and sycamore using medium-gauge stub wires. Use fine wire for smaller foliage. Thread the wire in and out vertically through each leaf, close to the central vein, like taking a large tacking stitch in needlework. If the loose end of the wire isn't long enough to fix to a branch or press into foam, twist another one around it to lengthen it. Bind the wire stem with green gutta-percha tape.

FOLIAGE FRAMES

Wind fresh foliage stems around picture and mirror frames to create trails of greenery. Evergreen foliage such as ivy, herbs such as rosemary and sage, and hop bines with their cone-like bracts, all last well and make good long-term decorations. Outline a kitchen mirror frame with herb stems or buy bunches of hops from the florist to soften the harsh silhouette of the top of a kitchen cupboard or window-frame. Make sure though that you can still open the cupboard door or window.

For a short-lived decoration or a special effect for a party, use trails of deciduous leaves to adorn the room. Copper beech will add a touch of burnished gold, effective against a light wood such as pine. Supple' stems of weeping willow suits curved and circular shapes.

FURTHER FOLIAGE SUGGESTIONS

It is challenging to create floral arrangements using only a mixture of foliage and perhaps including the green bracts of bells of Ireland and the dome-like heads of euphorbia. Select a few types of foliage from the garden, house plants or stems from the florist. Perhaps include long, pointed green iris leaves, clumps of silver-grey, slender carnation foliage, and purplish rose leaves to make an upright arrangement in a shallow dish.

You can arrange foliage to suit any mood and style, just as you would with flowers. A white jug with a simple bunch of variegated periwinkle, blue-grey rue, golden feverfew and feathery tansy leaves would capture attention.

For a more formal effect, you could create a triangular foliage design in an urn-shaped vase, using round and frilled leaves such as geranium and lady's mantle and the geometric seedheads of sea holly and globe thistle. Make your selection with a wide variety of shape, texture and colour, to avoid a heavy design of all dark, matt foliage types.

The two arrangements featured here show a couple of examples of what different effects can be achieved using foliage.

The design in the wicker basket is quite permanent as the plants are all growing. They can either all be transplanted into potting compost in the waterproofed basket or left in individual pots and wedged firmly into place. The tops of the pots can then be concealed with moss. One clear advantage of constructing the arrangement in this fashion is that should one of the chosen plants wilt or die it can be easily replaced without having to disturb the roots of the other plants. Another advantage of this display is that if it is well tended to it will last for a few months.

The arrangement in the glass container has a more sophisticated, airy feel. The base of the bowl is partially filled with white, clear and pale-coloured marbles. The arrangement of trailing ivy and assorted house plants is inserted into soaked florist foam that has been securely taped into the mouth of the bowl. This arrangement will last for a long time if kept well watered.

The design is a good illustration of the interesting effect that can be achieved by combining foliage of varied colours and textures, for example in the way that the central stems of variegated ivy trails across the dark, glossy fatsia leaf that forms the focal point.

Decorative Herbs

Fresh herbs are enormously versatile, combining attractive flowers with sweet and refreshing aromas that can be used in a variety of exciting displays. You can create instant effects with a herb arrangement just by standing a bushy basil plant on a sunny windowsill or displaying a mass of fennel seedheads in a simple white jug. As the finishing touch to a long, cool drink, add ice cubes set around bright blue borage flowers or tiny sprigs of fresh bright green mint. They are also very handy to have in the house as they add zest to many recipes, so your attractive arrangements have a practical use too.

GROWING HERBS INDOORS
Luckily, herbs are among the easiest of plants to grow, since most of them are native to Mediterranean countries where they are used to poor, but well-drained soil and warm, dry conditions. This makes them the ideal choice for first-time indoor gardeners.

It's best to buy small container-grown plants, usually raised in flexible plastic or fibre pots to create an instant indoor garden. Choose bushy, compact plants with plenty of side growth.

Herb plants will probably come with a care label giving basic growing and maintenance instructions. There are a few important points to remember when growing herbs. They enjoy a sunny position, so move them to a south-facing windowsill remembering to turn them occasionally so that they don't grow lopsidedly towards the source of light. Stand them outside occasionally if they are normally positioned away from the full sun. They also respond to regular feeding – a few drops of plant food added to the water once a week promotes healthy growth. Finally, because of their hot, dry origins, herb plants will not tolerate being over-watered. Provide plenty of fresh air.

Whatever grouping you make, whether it is on a windowsill or dining table, choose a selection of herbs that contrast well in aroma, flavour and appearance. A good collection to begin with would be curly and flat-leaved parsley varieties. Chunky clumps of slender chives, variegated applemint, bright golden marjoram, purple-pointed, oval-leaved basil and trailing thyme.

THE RIGHT CONTAINER
The choice of containers is as important for plants as it is for flowers: more so, perhaps, since a growing decoration lasts longer. Although they are simple and practical, earthenware flower pots can also look decorative, especially when they are grouped on a basketweave tray or a shallow wooden box. Don't forget to stand each pot on a non-porous saucer or dish, or to line a large container with an unobtrusive waterproof dish. Alternatively, place your pot inside another container, standing on a layer of gravel. You can then remove and replace the plant easily if it gets too big or needs a spell outside to recuperate. Plant individual herbs in simple plastic flower pots and conceal them in containers such as beakers, mugs, pottery mustard pots and preserve jars, old ginger jars and small pie dishes.

A similar selection of herbs makes an attractive indoor garden, planted in one or two large, shallow casseroles, in pottery bulb bowls or a plastic-lined basket.

HERBS AND FLOWERS
Herb flowers may not be the showiest blooms, but they all have their own delicate charm: rosemary with tiny blue flowers at the base of needle-like leaves: the bright blue star-like blooms of borage: chives, with pinky-mauve domes carried high above the vertical leaves: the minute pink or white flowers of scented geranium; fennel with umbrella-shaped heads of bright yellow: and the bright pink or mauve flowers of sage and marjoram with thick trusses of mauve flowers.

You can create delightful effects by grouping together jugs of individual flowering herbs – a jug of yellow fennel towering over a handful of pink-flowering spearmint and creamy-yellow comfrey. Or you can compose the small-flowering herbs to make a soft and pretty leafy background for more showy yellow nasturtiums and other garden flowers.

DISPLAY IDEAS
A pot of pinky-mauve flowering herbs, some long and spiky, some bushy and rounded, looks even better if you add toning cosmos flowers, a few pink roses and a cluster of border pinks. A jug of yellow and white flowering herbs comes into sharper focus if you accentuate it with a few stems of sweet-scented green and white flowering tobacco plants and a few yellow-centred marguerites.

Some of the larger herb plants such as fennel, dill and coriander produce large and plentiful umbrella-shaped flowers and seedheads and the more stems you cut, the more flowers will develop, giving you a ready supply throughout the summer. The architectural quality of a bunch of these tall, flowering stems is best displayed in an upright, slender container against a plain wall. Positioned in front of a window, they filter the light most attractively. Herbs can also mix well with other flowers.

VICTORIAN DELIGHTS
An innovative way of using herbs is to emulate a Victorian idea. They were among the first to appreciate the charms of herbs and foliage as distinct arranging materials, separate from flowers.

They often created elaborate leafy centrepieces and also enjoyed making fragrant herbs into little bunches to form unusual, aromatic and attractive displays for dinner-party tables.

Fragrant Herb Nosegays

IMBUE A SUMMER LUNCHEON WITH THE ATMOSPHERE OF A SUMMER GARDEN BY GRACING YOUR
TABLE WITH THESE SCENTED HERB AND FLOWER NOSEGAYS

These individual herb and flower posies form a fresh and attractive finishing touch to a lunch-party table. They make a refreshing change from identical table displays and add to the sense of occasion. Alternate posies by featuring a pink display at each lady's place setting and a blue flower design for the gentlemen.

CHOOSING THE FOLIAGE
Culinary herbs provide most of the foliage shown. If you have a herb garden, it will be at its best in the summer. You also can buy a wide selection of fresh herbs from a market or supermarket. The leaves can get squashed in their cling-wrapped packets, so buy the herbs the day before, unwrap them, re-cut their stems and place them loosely in a glass of water. This gives the herbs time to assume a more natural-looking shape. Conditioning the herbs overnight will make the featured arrangements more long-lasting.

Fresh mint, lemon thyme and sage are featured in the woman's posy. There are many suitable mint species and cultivars, such as spearmint, pineapple mint, horse mint, apple mint and water mint. Pineapple mint has attractive, grey-green and white variegated leaves, and variegated ginger mint has lovely, yellow-splashed leaves.

Lemon thyme has delicate green, silver or gold-variegated foliage, according to cultivar. Plain or variegated garden thyme, summer or winter savory, or sprigs of rockery-plant foliage, such as aubretia, origanum or alyssum could be substituted.

Common grey garden sage is shown, but there are purple and yellow-leaved sages, and 'Tricolor' sage with leaves attractively splashed in white, purple, pink and green. In place of these, use Jerusalem sage (*Phlomis fruitcosa*) or dead-nettle foliage.

Anaphalis, a herbaceous perennial with white, bauble-like everlasting flowers, can help to add textural contrast with its soft, grey leaves. As an alternative, you could also use *Senecio greyi* 'Sunshine' foliage.

MASCULINE FRAGRANCE
For the man's posy, rosemary, delicately scented geranium and *Stachys lanata* (lamb's tongue) foliage is used. A small-leaved hebe would give a spiky, rosemary-like effect, or use sprigs of lavender foliage. You could use anaphalis or *S. greyi* 'Sunshine' instead of the lamb's tongue.

There are dozens of old-fashioned scented geraniums, which correctly should be called pelargoniums, with fragrance varying from lemon and tea rose to pepper; the foliage varies from large, solid, round leaves to those resembling delicate lace. The softly pleated leaves of lady's mantle could also be used as a substitute.

CHOOSING THE FLOWERS
The posy settings are distinguished further by the different coloured feature blooms. Pink garden roses and hardy, herbaceous perennial geraniums (as opposed to tender geraniums, or pelargoniums) are used in the woman's posy. You could coax open a florist's pink rose instead, or use florist's spray roses which would help to create the feeling of sitting in a garden. Tightly bunched pink spray carnations would also give this feeling, more so than large-flowered, single pink carnations which could still be used. Single pink, fully-open paeonies would be lovely, but allow them time to mature if you buy them in bud.

Large-flowered hybrid clematis in a blue-mauve shade is the focal point of the man's posy, with love-in-a-mist in a supporting role. Clematis is not available as a cut flower; if you don't grow it, use blue-china asters, agapanthus, brodiaea, scabious or a cluster of globe thistles instead. Clematis may wilt unless conditioned properly; put the cut stem ends in boiling water for a few seconds and give them a long drink.

Love-in-a-mist is a cheerful summer florist's flower; buy a large bunch and air dry the remaining flowers. Cornflowers, bachelor's buttons on the other hand, would help to reinforce the masculine theme in the man's display.

CHOOSING THE CONTAINERS
If you can use the same glass pattern for the posies and for the wine, it gives a pleasing sense of continuity to the table display. Mixing and matching can be just as successful. Stemmed glass dessert bowls were used for the featured displays.

Standard Paris wine goblets, or long, narrow flutes, which widen towards the top, would also look effective. If the supply of flowers and foliage allow, you could do dramatic individual posies for each place setting in huge, balloon-shaped brandy goblets. Make sure there's plenty of table space so the flowers and foliage are not overhanging the plates of food.

DISPLAY VARIATIONS
The ideal setting is a dining room table, but you could vary the arrangement of the glasses to suit the exact shape of the table. On a very narrow table, you could place the posies in a line down the middle, or form a tight circle in the centre of a round table, instead of putting one at each place setting. Luncheon parties don't always have an equal number of male and female guests, so it may be better to have a central display rather than emphasize this.

MAKING THE FEMININE POSY

INGREDIENTS
1 glass dessert bowl
2 one pink garden rose
3 one bunch of mint
4 four stems of hardy pink geranium
5 six sprigs of lemon thyme
6 one bunch of common garden sage
7 one bunch of anaphalis

LEFT A pink garden rose is the focus of the woman's posy. Foliage from herbs adds mass and fragrance; hardy geranium flowers echo the pink theme.

1 Arrange the anaphalis around the rim of the bowl. Next, add the sage so that the bushy leaves help fill out the bowl. Trim three stems of this herb to about the same length as the anaphalis. Use the sage stems to help establish the all-round posy shape of the display, by placing them between the anaphalis. Again, criss-cross their stem ends to provide a firm base for the other ingredients.

2 Trim down four or five stems of mint so each individual stem is about 5cm (2 in) long. Arrange the mint among the anaphalis and the sage. This will add variety of shape, colour and scent to the predominantly green foliage. Introduce sprigs of lemon thyme amongst the other herbs; you will require about six sprigs to create an impact.

3 Choose a perfect pink garden rose, removing the damaged outer petals if necessary. Trim off any leaves and thorns and cut the stem to a length of 5cm (2 in). Position it in the centre of the dessert bowl to form your centrepiece. To finish off, trim four hardy pink geranium stems to a length of 5cm (2 in) and arrange them around the outer edge of the bowl.

MAKING THE MASCULINE POSY

INGREDIENTS
1 *glass dessert bowl*
2 *one blue clematis bloom*
3 *one bunch of rosemary*
4 *three scented geranium leaves*
5 *three stems of love-in-a-mist*
6 *four sprigs of lamb's tongue*

LEFT Blue love-in-a-mist and clematis set the tonal theme for the masculine posy; rosemary's geranium leaves and lamb's tongue provide the fragrant fillers.

1 Arrange the trimmed sprigs of lambs tongue into a circle around the edge of the bowl. Take five sprigs of rosemary, remove the lower foliage and cut the stems to a length of 8cm (3 in). Place them around the edge of the bowl among the lamb's tongue leaves for contrast in texture and fragrance. The rosemary should stand taller than the lamb's tongue leaves to show its foliage.

2 Remove three individual variegated scented geranium leaves from a single stem. Choose them for their perfect formation and young-green colouring. An odd number of leaves are used so the arrangement doesn't become too symmetrical. Position them carefully among the other foliage, making sure their stems reach the water.

3 Choose a perfect blue clematis flower to form the focus of the display. Trim the stem to a length of 5cm (2in). Arrange it so the flower sits comfortably in the centre of the posy. Lastly, add three stems of pale blue love-in-a-mist. Remove the spindly leaves cut to 8cm (3in) and arrange around the central bloom.

Vegetable Variety

THE HUMBLE MARROW FORMS THE BASE FOR THIS EXOTIC-LOOKING

DISPLAY OF HALLOWE'EN BOUNTY

This display will transform the most 'spur of the moment' event into an occasion to remember.

The display is asymmetrical, front-facing and made from fresh flowers, branches, seed pods and berries arranged in a hollowed-out marrow.

CHOOSING THE FLOWERS
Typical late summer and autumn flowers are used in rich variations of orange.

Gladioli should be cheap and in good supply during the late summer. Orange-rimmed yellow gladioli are shown; you may have to order these in advance, or use all-orange or yellow gladioli. Alternatively, use several stems of orange tiger lilies.

Yarrow, or achillea, sometimes can be ordered through a florist. It may be easier to buy dried achilleas; use freshly dried for a strong yellow colour.

EXOTIC KNIPHOFIA
Red-hot poker, also called torch lily or kniphofia, is a dramatic end-of-summer flower. As well as the golden-orange form shown, there are fiery red, scarlet, lemon yellow and bi-coloured cultivars. You may be able to order kniphofia from a florist, but they could be expensive, however, only four stems are needed for this composition. Buy kniphofias when the lower florets are open or starting to show colour; these continue to open for several days.

Kniphofias continue to grow in water, and this gives an unusual, attractive aspect. If you can't obtain kniphofia, use orange foxtail lily (*Eremerus bungei*).

BEAUTIFUL ALTERNATIVES
Montbretia, or crocosmia, is another old-fashioned plant. There are named cultivars in the same yellow, orange and red colour range as kniphofias, and bi-colours, but vivid orange is the most common type.

Antholyza, or 'Aunt Eliza', is a similar plant, with elegant spikes of vivid orange, funnel-shaped flowers in late summer.

Carthamus, also called safflower, adds density and intense splashes of orange. You could use French marigolds.

Haemanthus, or blood lily, is the most unusual flower called for. They are South African bulbous plants, related to amaryllis and sometimes grown as house plants. You may be able to order haemanthus through your florist; if so, re-cut the stems under water, then give them a long, cold drink for

PREPARING THE VEGETABLE BASE

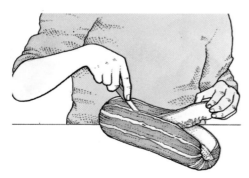

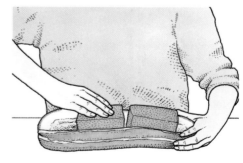

1 Turn the vegetable round until you find a side on which it rests steadily on a flat surface. Otherwise, trim a few thin layers of skin from one side to give the marrow a flat base. Using a sharp knife, cut out a 'V' shaped section along the length of the vegetable.

2 Scoop out the inside of the vegetable with a spoon. Try to remove as much flesh as possible, but take care not to make the shell too flimsy. When most of the flesh has been removed, use a blunt knife to give the inside a smoother surface.

3 Cut a small block of florist's foam into sections. Push them into the hollowed-out section of the vegetable. Fill any small gaps with foam cut-offs so that it is filled completely with foam. Trim the top of the foam until it is level with the rim of the vegetable.

MAKING AN ARRANGEMENT IN A HOLLOWED-OUT VEGETABLE

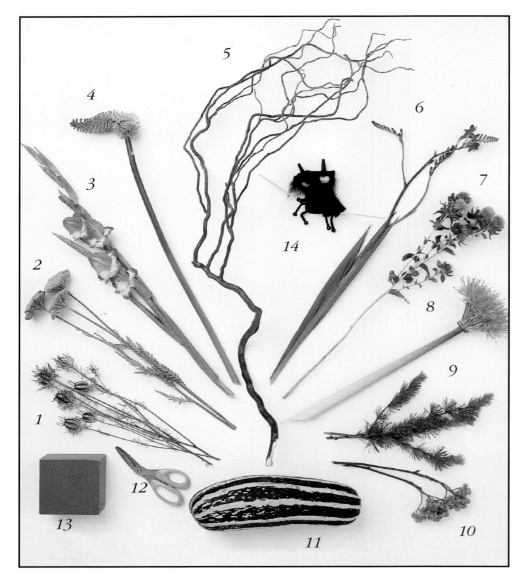

1 Prepare a base from a marrow at least 32cm (13 in) long, (see box). Cut a piece of contorted willow to 75cm (30 in) then cut the stem at a slant. Place the twig to the right in the base. Insert four or five sprigs of the larch foliage at one end of the foam, and the rest in a vertical grouping at the base of the willow stem.

4 Cut three stems of montbretia at graduated lengths. Insert them into the foam to the side of the gladioli. Turn the flowers so they face outwards. Trim the stems from one bunch of love-in-a-mist to varying lengths, and group them to one side of the base. Make a low-lying group of love-in-a-mist seed pods and insert on the other side.

INGREDIENTS

1 1 bunch of love-in-a-mist
2 9 stems of yarrow
3 3 stems of gladiolus
4 3 stems of red-hot poker (kniphofia)
5 1 contorted willow stem
6 3 stems of montbretia
7 1 bunch of carthamus

8 2 stems of haemanthus
9 3-4 stems of larch foliage
10 5 stems of sorbus berries
11 1 marrow
12 scissors
13 1 block of florist's foam
14 2 novelty witches

2 Cut three gladiolus stems, the longest to 56cm (22 in), and the other two slightly shorter. Again, cut the stems at an angle for easy insertion into the foam. Position them in a tight group alongside the contorted twig. Add the novelty witches in between the twigs and gladioli.

3 Cut two red-hot poker stems and insert them in the middle of the foliage. Cut a bent flowerhead slightly shorter than the other two and insert it next to the others. Cut one haemanthus stem just underneath the flowerhead. Insert it at the base of the gladiolus stems. Cut another haemanthus stem, and insert alongside the gladioli.

5 Break off the short stems from eight stems of carthamus. Strip off the lower leaves and group them at both ends of the marrow base, at the same level as the haemanthus bloom. Place a few more stems at the base of the display. Cut nine stems of yarrow to graduated heights. Arrange them in a group centrally.

6 Cut the stems of the sorbus berries to 13cm (5 in). Cut the woody stems at a slant. Insert them in a row along the base of foam. Place them so clusters of berries cascade over the rim of the marrow base. Check for any gaps. Fill in any exposed areas with sprigs of larch foliage at the front and with stems of montbretia at the back.

several hours. Good alternatives include several clustered stems of nerine, or Guernsey lily.

CHOOSING SEED PODS AND BERRIES

Seed pods and berries add contrast in scale and rich, textural detail.

Love-in-a-mist, or nigella, seed pods are shown, but pot marigold, burdock or 'Paper Moon' scabious seedheads could be used instead. Burdock and 'Paper Moon' scabious both need careful handling.

Sorbus, or rowan, berries are as attractive to birds as they are to flower arrangers. If the berries have been eaten use cotoneaster or pyracantha berries, or garden or wild rose hips.

CHOOSING THE FOLIAGE AND BRANCHES

Larch foliage helps integrate the display, carrying the green of the marrow up and through the flowers. You could use pine, eucalyptus, blue spruce or leather leaf fern from the florists.

Contorted, Peking or curly willow has a flowing growth habit, and it adds a sense of movement to a display. Here, it sets the height and counteracts the perfect straightness of the achillea and kniphofia stems. You could use contorted hazel instead, or ordinary hazel or birch.

CHOOSING THE CONTAINER

A marrow makes a natural vase since it is waterproof and the high moisture content helps prevent the florist's foam block from drying out. Try to choose a marrow without any soft spots or blemishes.

The marrow shown is 35cm (14 in) long. Melons are related to marrows; a scooped-out canteloup or watermelon also would make a suitable container.

CHOOSING THE SETTING

A buffet table, drinks table or hall table would be ideal, perhaps with a collection of small ornamental gourds nearby, in a shallow wooden bowl. Alternatively, give it more emphasis with lit candles – a sense of grandeur for adults, and a reference to the spooky and tingling excitement of Hallowe'en for children.

Medley Display

THIS KITCHEN DISPLAY OF FRESH FRUIT, SUCCULENT VEGETABLES AND VIVID

FLOWERS MAKES AN INNOVATIVE STATEMENT

This breakfast-time project is an informal, all-round display, made from attractive salad vegetables, fruit, flowers and foliage. The ingredients are built up tightly on a foundation of saturated florist's foam previously encased in chicken wire and fixed to a round, wooden breadboard.

CHOOSING THE VEGETABLES
Most of the fruit and vegetables shown are readily available from greengrocers and street market stalls, and the unusual ones are sold in larger supermarkets, ethnic food shops and specialist stores. Try to look out for perfect, unblemished specimens to include in your display.

Twelve small tomatoes are impaled onto stub wires covered with gutta-percha tape and used to provide bulk in the display. Firm tomatoes are essential, otherwise they will split when impaled; if you have the choice, select slightly green, unripe ones. They will ripen quickly at room temperature.

Radishes, with their fresh green leaves, add low-level interest round the base. If you can only get leafless radishes, tuck sprigs of weeping fig, eucalyptus or ivy foliage under each one to set off their deep red colour.

Silver pickling onions, once their papery skins are removed, look like outsized pearls. Here, they are wired onto false stems and used to add stark highlights to the display. Small button mushrooms, or eight to ten small garlic bulbs could be used instead.

USING CHILLIES
Fresh red chillies are wired into flower-like bunches and inserted randomly. Their long, tapering form gives the design an interesting silhouette. Yellow and glossy-green chillies also are available, so you could use a mixture of all three. It's a good idea to wear gloves when handling chillies because they can cause skin irritation; never touch or rub your eyes when handling chillies, and always wash your hands afterwards.

One red and one yellow pepper are cut into quarters so the shiny outsides and seed-filled insides are on display. You also could use a traditional green pepper, half-ripe peppers, with streaks of yellow, orange, red and green; or the more unusual purple-black peppers.

Artichoke heads are unripe buds, and the leaf-like bracts are the edible parts. For a similar solid, round form, use large purple Spanish onions or even ordinary onions, supported on wooden dowels. Kumquats are citrus fruits, but their bright

MAKING A BASE

Secure a prong to the centre of the chopping board with florist's adhesive clay. Cut a small cube and a larger, rounded mound from a block of florist's foam and attach the smaller piece to the top of the larger one with stub wires. Wrap in chicken wire and impale onto the prong to make a firm base.

orange colour fits in beautifully with the vegetables. In fact, peppers, tomatoes and chillies also are technically fruits because they contain seeds, but they are referred to as vegetables, as they're used in savoury dishes.

CHOOSING THE FLOWERS
Purple spikes of herbaceous veronica set the height and form a fountain-like top to the display. Hebe, or shrubby veronica, could be used, or short lengths of fuchsia. For an unusual effect, use the smokey seedheads of the smoke bush, *Cotinus coggygria*.

Rudbeckia, or cone flower, is also known as 'Black-eyed Susan', because of its black, mounded, velvety centres. Any daisy-like flower, such as marguerite, chrysanthemum, aster, coreopsis or cosmos, could be substituted.

No other flower has the same intricate appearance as cockscomb, but you could use broccoli or quartered sections of cauliflower instead. Both have a texture and mass similar to cockscomb. Buy the broccoli and cauliflower with buds as small and tightly closed as possible.

Hypericum, or St John's wort, has stopped flowering by late summer, and is in its berrying stage. You could use rosehips instead, or sprigs of blackberries, rowanberries or elderberries.

CHOOSING THE FOLIAGE
Boston fern fronds form a lacy collar round the base. If you have a large Boston fern house plant, take the fronds from the base, where they're less likely to be missed. Otherwise, use florist's leather leaf, asparagus fern foliage or 20cm (8 in) sprigs from an ivy or tradescantia plant.

Fresh parsley is used as a filler foliage. Parsley is widely available, but try to buy

MAKING YOUR FRUIT AND VEGETABLE DISPLAY

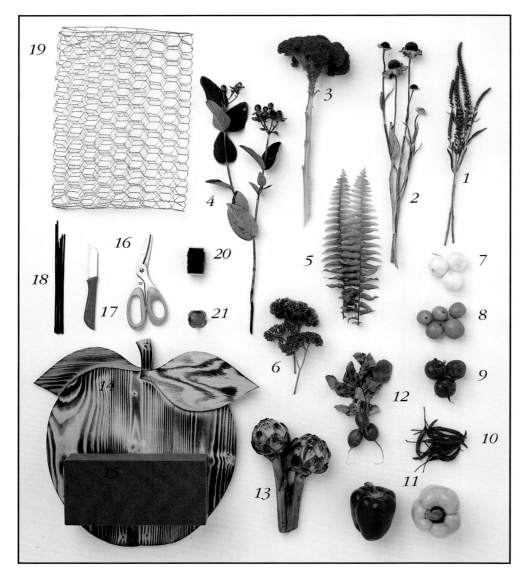

1 Make the foam base (see box). Cut ten Boston fern leaves from a house plant. Insert them at even intervals around the base of the foam to make a low-lying collar of foliage. Cut five baby artichoke heads, leaving a thick length of stem, 15cm (6 in) long. Cut the stems to a slant. Group two heads together on one side of the display, three on the other.

4 Place the radishes around the base of the display with the leaves hanging over the rim. Position the rest at the top of the arrangement to nestle amongst the other materials. Attach them to the top of the display by pushing them into the chicken wire. Wire up eight to ten kumquats. Insert them randomly around the display.

INGREDIENTS

1 15 stems of veronica
2 14-16 stems of rudbeckia
3 4 stems of cockscomb
4 15 sprigs of hypericum
5 10 Boston fern leaves
6 bunch of parsley
7 18-20 silver onions
8 8-10 kumquats
9 12 tomatoes
10 32 chilli peppers
11 1 red and 1 yellow pepper
12 1 bunch of radishes
13 5 artichoke heads
14 wooden chopping board
15 block of florist's foam
16 scissors
17 knife
18 tape-covered wires
19 chicken wire
20 fine reel wire
21 prong

2 Cut four stems of bright red cockscomb flowers to a length of 15cm (6 in). Insert two stems, one above the other, at the front, and two at the back of the display. Strip away the outside papery covering from the silver onions and wire them individually. Insert 18-20 wired onions in small groups all around the arrangement.

3 Cut one red pepper and one yellow pepper into quarters. Wire up some quarters and insert. Attach the rest by pushing firmly onto the chicken wire. Turn some pieces round to show the inside, and others to show the skins. Cut off sprigs of hypericum berries. Make a collar above the fern. Insert one at the top of the display.

5 Break off sprigs of parsley and insert them around the display, linking the larger flowerheads and vegetables with small patches of green. Wire together a bunch of four or five chilli peppers and insert them evenly around the display. Strip the lower leaves from 15 stems of veronica. Insert them vertically into the top of the arrangement.

6 Tape over 12 thick gauge stub wires with gutta-percha tape. Spear the ends of 12 small tomatoes. Insert them into the foam base so that they are raised above the other ingredients. Cut 16 stems of rudbeckia to a length of 8cm (3in). Insert them around the upright veronica stems. Add a few more stems of rudbeckia.

unwrapped bunches, as the Cellophane wrapping often used by supermarkets can conceal wilted foliage. When you get the parsley home, re-cut the stems, submerge it for a few minutes in cold water, then place in a jar or glass of water and keep refrigerated until needed.

CHOOSING THE SETTING

The display is shown on a kitchen table, but it also would make a lovely centrepiece for a lunch or dinner party, either indoors in the dining room or outdoors in the garden. If you're having people round for drinks, and serving raw vegetables and dips, you could place the raw vegetables in small dishes, arranged around the display but you'll have to make sure any children present do not start to dismantle the display and eat it.

The arrangement would also make an attractive and appropriate display for a harvest festival in chapel or church, or as a centrepiece at a harvest supper. You could place the arrangement on a wide bench-seat in a church porch, on a table or wooden chest, or even on a wide recessed windowsill, where the brilliant colours would be seen to advantage. To give the tomatoes and peppers added highlights, polish them with a soft dry cloth before completing the arrangement and, if you wish, brush them lightly with vegetable oil.

LOOKING AFTER THE DISPLAY

This is a short-lived display, because summer heat hastens the ripening process of fruit and vegetables, and if cut or pierced, as here, they mature much quicker. Give the display a regular spray-misting with water to keep it looking fresh.

As the soaked florist's foam is placed on a wooden board, you cannot easily pour on water to keep it permanently moist. But you can remove some of the flowers, and the parsley, and give them a reviving drink in water overnight. Then cut a short length from the stem end before repositioning it in the foam.

Dry the artichokes for everlasting displays; stuff tissue paper between the bracts to keep them open as they dry and put them in a well ventilated location and out of direct sunlight.

Formal Fruit Display

THIS LUSCIOUS ARRAY OF SUMPTUOUS FLOWERS, TROPICAL FRUIT AND FOLIAGE MAKES
A MOUTH-WATERING BUFFET TABLE DISPLAY FOR A SPECIAL OCCASION

This striking 'helter-skelter' of fruit and flowers will attract everyone's attention so give it pride of place on the buffet table at an engagement, birthday or anniversary party. Only a few stems of each flower type are required so this splendid display can look extravagant without being expensive. Choose a range of standard, brightly coloured flowers and concentrate on an unusual collection of nuts and exotic tropical fruit.

CHOOSING RAINBOW HUES
The colour scheme of the featured display is a vivid mixture of bright tropical fruit and flowers in all the hues of the rainbow. Warm and hot colours predominate, with sunny yellows, pinks and oranges setting the tone, and cool purple, neutral beige and white providing contrast. You could interpret the idea in a single colour scheme, but it's both easier and more exciting to buy for a multi-colour display, and the finished effect looks more festive. Although some blue-dyed gypsophila is included, blue is not a colour normally associated with food, so use it with restraint.

Make the arrangement in its finished location so that you don't risk disturbing the display by moving it around. As some of the fruit needs to be sliced for display, and fruit stains are notoriously difficult to wash out, cover the tablecloth under your cutting board with something waterproof, such as a large plastic bag. Ordinary absorbent kitchen paper does not provide enough protection. Tuck the waterproof covering underneath the base of the stand so the cut fruit does not pass over any exposed tablecloth. Have a damp sponge handy to mop up any spilt juice.

Try to make up the display as close as possible to the beginning of the party as cut fruit surfaces discolour quickly and dry up. Painting the exposed surfaces with lemon juice helps prevent discolouration, as does covering the arrangement completely with kitchen plastic wrap before it goes on display.

CHOOSING THE RIGHT FLOWERS AND FOLIAGE
A mixture of garden and florist's material is used, but the choice of flowers is flexible. If you have a garden, you could still achieve striking effects with just garden flowers and foliage. Make sure that the material to be used has rigid stems for insertion into the florist's foam foundation, and will be resilient enough to stay fresh-looking for several hours.

Florist's yellow spray roses are featured, but they could be replaced easily with garden roses. If you are working to a budget, buy double chrysanthemums but go for a clear range of colours, avoiding autumn russets.

Pale-pink florist's stocks and spray carnations provide both fragrance and frilly textural interest. Pink spray carnations are inexpensive, and one bunch should be enough, but garden pinks or sweet williams are possible alternatives. Avoid large, single carnations as they're out of scale with the rest of the display. Evergreen spurge (*Euphorbia robbiae*) is a valuable garden plant that has flower-like basal rosettes of shiny, dark-green leaves and long-lasting flower bracts. Here, it's used to give a strong vertical accent to the display. Your florist may be able to supply evergreen spurge if you order it in advance; otherwise, use caper spurge, lady's mantle, or florist's pittosporum. (See the box for important information on using spurge in arrangements.)

A mixed colour selection of florist's Turk's-cap ranunculus feature in the display. They could be replaced with garden roses, double geums or trollius. Yellow freesias make unusual filler flowers as freesias are rarely used on such short stems in displays. You could use pink or purple freesias, or tightly packed heads of azaleas or viburnums.

Feverfew, or matricaria, is a shortlived perennial chrysanthemum that seeds itself freely in gardens. Any similar, daisy-like flower, such as anthemis, English daisy or small, single, white florist's chrysanthemums could be substituted; later in the year, asters would be ideal. The alternative flowers must be dainty, or they'll overpower the display.

FLEXIBLE STEMS
Weeping willow branches are wound in ribbon-like spirals around the display. Any other malleable stem, such as honeysuckle, ivy, clematis, jasmine or ornamental or edible grape vine could be used instead. Florist's asparagus fern is another alternative, or you could cut sprigs from an *Asparagus sprengeri* house plant. As a last resort use a long, trailing stem of spider plant, complete with plantlets.

Pieris is a hardy evergreen shrub with flowers similar to lily of the valley. In fact it's a member of the *Ericaceae* family, and related to rhododendron and heather. Your florist may be able to order some for you, but it won't be cheap, as it's slow growing and only bears heavy crops of flowers when mature. The related arbutus, or strawberry tree, with white, bell-like flowers could be used instead. Stems of wisteria or laburnum also will create a similar weeping effect. Once cut, both last better without their foliage.

Lastly, eucalyptus provides unusual, reddish flowers, as well as its familiar grey

CREATING A FRUIT AND FLOWER DISPLAY

1 Stick two prongs to the base of the cake stand with adhesive clay. Trim the edges of a block of foam to make a pyramid shape. Criss-cross tape over the foam, bringing the two pieces over each side of the cake stand. Hook lengths of wire around three bananas and attach. Press sprigs of eucalyptus into the foam between the lower bananas.

4 Cut flowering sprigs of stocks and insert them in a tightly bunched group between the aubergine (eggplant) slices. Cut four or five stems of pinks underneath the flowerhead and insert in a mass above the stock. Cut six to eight stems of freesias leaving a short stem. Insert them into the foam in a low-lying group with three wired lemon slices in a row above.

INGREDIENTS

1 2 stems of matricaria
2 3 stems of weeping willow
3 3 stems of evergreen spurge
4 8-10 stems of ranunculus
5 2-3 stems of gypsophila, blue-dyed
 and natural
6 5 stems of pinks
7 6-8 stems of freesia
8 3 stems of spray roses
9 3 stems of pieris

10 2 stems of flowering eucalyptus
11 2 stems of stock
12 strip of adhesive clay
13 A selection of fruits and nuts
14 stub wires
15 2 prongs
16 adhesive tape
17 scissors
18 florist's foam
19 pedestal cake stand

2 Cut the stems of eight to ten roses about 6cm (2½ in) from the flowerhead and press into the foam. Cut three long slices from an aubergine (eggplant) and remove the inside flesh so that the slices lies flat against the foam. Bend three lengths of wire into hairpin shapes. Place each aubergine (eggplant) slice against the foam. Attach to the foam with wire.

3 Cut the stems from eight to ten ranunculus just underneath the flowerhead. Press each one into the foam, filling the space between two slices of aubergine (eggplant). Insert a group of six to eight slices of wired star fruit (see box) above the ranunculus. Build up the group by overlapping the slices in a line.

5 Insert eight wired kumquats above the roses. Cut off sprigs of matricaria and insert into the foam above the kumquats. Make bunched florets of gypsophila and insert into the foam above the freesia. Top this with grapes, lychees and gooseberries. Insert three upright stems of evergreen spurge and walnuts and hazelnuts in a line above the kumquats.

6 Cut off three, long stems of pieris at a slant. Insert them at the top of the display. Place two or three strawberries underneath the pieris and the same number at the base of the cake stand. Cut the peel from two satsumas to make a spiral and hang it over the edge. Insert one end of three long willow stems into the foam and wind them round the display in a spiral to finish.

foliage; most florists carry a year-round supply. Otherwise, use the grey-leaved *Senecio greyi* 'Sunshine'.

CHOOSING THE FRUIT

With today's sophisticated interest in food, many supermarkets stock a wide range of tropical fruits as well as more ordinary varieties. Often, too, local outdoor markets have stalls brimming with colourful exotic fruits and vegetables.

Take your time when shopping and buy only perfect fruit. If you are not satisfied, choose a substitute fruit or even vegetable; the distinction between the two is irrelevant in this display. Unusual tropical fruit is expensive but, as with the flowers, you only need a few specimens of each type.

Grapes have long been associated with festivities, perhaps because of their alcoholic by-products. Green, or 'white' grapes are shown but you could use red or black grapes instead.

The citrus family is well represented, with kumquats, lemons and satsumas, Kumquats look like miniature oranges. Sometimes they are grown as house plants for their fragrant flowers and glossy leaves, although they won't fruit indoors except under ideal conditions. Kumquats have a bitter, but refreshing, taste when eaten fresh. If you can't get kumquats, use grapes instead, but choose a different sort from those used already in the display.

Lemons are always available but limes look more unusual. Instead of satsumas, use tangerines and clementines: all were Christmas-time treats originally, but are widely available now from autumn through to early summer.

Cape gooseberries are related to the bright-orange Chinese lanterns used in dried-flower displays and the gooseberries can be eaten fresh or preserved. Here, they are used with their papery outer coverings, (calyces) still attached.

Aubergine, (eggplant), is technically a fruit, since it contains seeds, but is cooked as a vegetable. Its glossy purple skin gives its name to a popular fashion colour, and there is also a white-skinned variety, hence the name eggplant. Aubergine is related to potato and tomato, and to Cape gooseberry; they all belong to the *Solanaceae* family. Only the skin is used for the display, but you can put the scooped-out flesh to good culinary use. Buy the largest, shiniest aubergine you can find.

OUT OF THE ORDINARY

Star fruit, or carambola, is the most unusual ingredient. It has five distinct ribs creating star-shaped cross-sections. There is no other fruit to match star fruit, but cross-sections of kiwi fruit with its bright-green flesh and central ring of black seeds would look just as attractive.

Tinned lychees are the staple dessert of Chinese restaurants, but here the tropical fruit is used fresh in its rough pink outer shell. Lychee pips germinate freely, but the young plants need high humidity to thrive. Like kumquats, lychees are sold by weight, and only a few are needed. If you can't get them, use cherries instead.

Strawberries are available all year round, but they are expensive out of their natural season. Raspberries, blackberries and similar cane fruits are too soft and small to use individually, though you could insert short lengths of cane with clusters of fruit attached at intervals.

HANDLE WITH CARE

Evergreen spurge (*Euphorbia tobbiae*) releases a sap when the stem ends are cut. This sap causes severe irritation to the skin and is especially harmful if it gets in the eyes. Always wash your hands thoroughly after handling spurge in the featured arrangement, particularly as it is intended for display on a buffet table which will be laden with food, you may prefer to use one of the suggested alternatives to spurge, such as lady's mantle or pittosporum.

If you do use spurge and want to eat some of the tempting exotic fruits used in the arrangement, be certain to wash each piece of fruit thoroughly before consumption. To be absolutely safe, only eat fruit that still has its skin on, such as satsumas, and be sure to peel them carefully.

CHOOSING THE CONTAINER

A clear glass, raised cake stand, 15cm (6 in) high and 20cm (8 in) across, is used as the display base. You could use a plain china cake stand but avoid those with detailed floral decorations that would detract from the tropical effect. The display could be built up on a flat plate, but the raised stand counteracts the visual weightiness, and additionally the curled satsuma peels would have to be left out.

Another suitable alternative would be a ham stand, which is usually made of plain white china and is similar to a cake stand except the top is slightly dished, rather than flat. You would need to insert the twists of citrus fruit peel a little above the base of the foam pyramid, so that they clear the rim of the stand and cascade attractively over it.

If you cannot obtain a pedestal stand of any kind, you could create a false pedestal by fixing a large, flat plate on to the top of a tall, sturdy china vase or, for a glowing alternative, a copper or brass plate to a tall metal vase.

Since the display itself is exceptionally tall, it is more important than ever that the method of fixing is sound and secure, to avoid the embarassment of any mishaps as guests reach across the buffet table to serve themselves from the surrounding dishes.

The supporting vase used to create a false pedestal must have a wide base, and be capacious enough to be filled with an

WIRING FRUIT AND NUTS

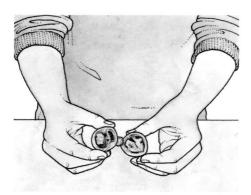

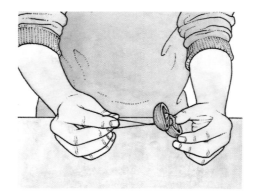

1 Insert a narrow blade along the seam of a walnut to split it cleanly into two equal halves. Fix a small blob of adhesive clay on one side and push the two halves of walnut together, both sides facing in the same direction.

2 Wrap a single fine stub wire around the blob of clay in the middle, taking care not to cut through the clay as you go. Twist the wire together to make a false stem to insert into the foam.

3 Insert a length of stub wire through the fat base of a small fruit such as kumquat, lychee grape or strawberry. Pull the wire halfway through the fruit and twist the two lengths together to form a false stem.

adequate amount of ballast. You can use sand, gravel, pebbles, stones or even damp soil. Once the vase is suitably weighted in this way, press a thick strip of florist's adhesive clay all around the rim, making sure that it is absolutely dry. It is important to use enough clay to give the plate a really firm grip. Place the plate centrally on the rim of the vase, and press firmly in position, pushing the clay on to the underside of the plate all around with your fingers.

CHOOSING THE SETTING

The centre of a buffet table is the ideal location for this display, but if there is a table for desserts. it could form the focal point there. Make sure there is plenty of space around the arrangement for guests to help themselves to food without knocking against it. Make sure, too, that there is plenty of fresh fruit on offer on conventional serving dishes, so no-one is tempted to pick any morsels from the display and spoil the effect.

LOOKING AFTER THE DISPLAY

This is a short-term arrangement, because cut fruit resting against saturated florist's foam soon rots in a warm room. Equally, the ethylene gas that is given off by fruit shortens the life of flowers such as gypsophila and freesia. After all the guests have gone, or the next morning, carefully take apart the display. Wash all the whole fruit thoroughly, as harmful sap from the spurge may have got to it, if you wish use to make a fruit salad. Discard all the cut sections of fruit.

Transfer the long-stemmed pieris and euphorbia to a tall vase. Carefully slice a round section from the base of the florist's foam to make an instant 'posy pad', and then you can insert the short-stemmed flowers for an attractive and long-lasting reminder of the occasion.

RIGHT The 'back' view is as beautiful as the front and, ideally, the arrangement should be seen in the round to enjoy the wealth of fruit and flowers on display.

CHAPTER FOUR

$\mathscr{D}$RIED FLOWERS

Dried flowers have long ago shaken off their dusty image, and are now proudly displayed all year round, not just as a poor, second-best substitute for fresh flowers in winter. The choice of commercially dried flowers is greater than ever, with local and exotic flowers from all over the world widely available from florists, gift shops, department stores, DIY and garden centres, either in mixed-flower bunches or single types.

Commercially dried flowers, foliage and seed pods come in natural colours, bleached and in a range of dyed hues, co-ordinated to complement the latest fashions in interior design, as well as basic primaries and neutrals. Ready-made arrangements are sold, but it's always nicer to create your own to exactly match your decor and express your personal style. Dried flower arrangements also make excellent, long-lasting gifts.

Working with dried flowers is perfect for learning about flower arranging: you can practice to your heart's content, reusing material over and over again, with no risk of it wilting or dying. Dried flowers are economical: one beautiful display can give pleasure for months, and you can refresh it by adding new material from time to time.

If you are fortunate enough to have a garden, you can grow flowers for drying. There are the so-called *immortelles*, the daisy-like, annual members of the *Compositae* family, such as strawflower and helipterum, plus other, easy, all-time favourites, such as statice, or annual sea lavender, Chinese lanterns and honesty, or

silver-moon. Many common place garden flowers also provide excellent material for drying: acanthus, yarrow, goldenrod, lady's mantle, globe thistle, sea holly, even peony and columbine seed heads.

Country walks can yield lovely dried flowers and seed pods of common 'weeds', such as cow parsley, or Queen Anne's lace, knotweed and ground elder. And urban waste ground is a good source: buddleia, rose-base willow herb and wild grass seed heads add character to even the dullest shop-bought dried material. Collecting and combining dried material from various sources encourages creativity and helps you achieve the exact 'look' you're after, as well as keeping you in touch with nature and the seasons – always a lovely bonus!

Air drying is the easiest and most common method of preserving material, but you can also replace natural sap with glycerine. Beech leaves are glycerined, but other leaves and a few flowers, such as bells of Ireland, also benefit from glycerine, which leaves the material flexible and life-like. A third option, ideal for delicate flowers, is drawing out their moisture with a desiccant, such as silica gel or borax, which retains the original colour perfectly. This chapter shows you how to use all three methods with easy-to-follow photographs, and also suggests the most suitable plants for each.

The main difference between working with fresh and dried flowers is the latter's stiff stems, which can look awkward, like the spokes of a bicycle wheel. Creating a natural, informal look is the most difficult

challenge, but we show you how to achieve this, with a minimum of effort and a great deal of pleasure.

In general terms, the stems of dried flowers, stripped of their thorns, and usually also of their leaves, add little if anything to the visual pleasure derived from a dried-flower arrangement. Further, some dried flowers need to be mounted on false stems of stub wires. Examples include the heads of strawflowers (see page 120) which all-too-readily snap off from their brittle stems once they are dried, and any flowers which have been dried in desiccant. It is usual to bind false wire stems with gutta percha tape in a tone that blends with the overall colour theme of the arrangement. But even so, whether they are naturally dried or bound wire, it is the stems which, to a large extent, determine the general principal of dried flower arranging.

Look carefully at any attractive display and you will notice that the flowers are positioned close together (though never so close that they squash or damage each other) so that the eye cannot travel between them, and the stems are completely hidden.

This full and tightly-packed appearance need not be unduly expensive in terms of flowers. Many of the prettiest arrangements make generous – though economic – use of the cheapest and most readily-available flower types, using them as a foil, or a natural background, to the more expensive or exotic examples, such as rosebuds and paeony blooms.

Air Drying Techniques

Allowing flowers and other plant materials to dry out in the air is the easiest and most popular method of preserving them. A wide variety of plant material can be dried using this process.

Although the principle of air drying remains the same whatever materials you use, the basic method can be adapted to suit individual foliage varieties.

PICKING PERFECT SPECIMENS

Select flowers that are in good condition, undamaged by insects or the weather. Pick them on a dry day, after the morning dew has dried and before the sun is at its hottest. If you do not have a garden, select perfect specimens from the florist.

Choose your drying area with care: It must be dry, cool – but no less than 10°C (50°F), well ventilated and the air should circulate freely; airing cupboards, attics, and garages usually meet these criteria – modern kitchens tend to be too hot and damp. Avoid hanging the flowers in direct sunlight as this causes colours to fade.

To achieve strong, natural colours in the dried material, it is important to make the drying period as short as possible. The time taken for flowers and foliage to dry completely depends on their density and size, the temperature, humidity and amount of air movement in the drying environment. The process is usually complete after four to ten days. The plant material is ready when it feels papery and rustles gently; seedheads should rattle.

THE HANGING METHOD

Hanging flowers in bunches, with their heads pointing downwards is used for the widest range of flowers, including everlasting flowers – members of the *Compositae* family – long-stemmed delphiniums, lavenders, heathers, mimosa and roses.

Before drying, check to make sure that the stems are in good condition. Remove any thorns and the lower leaves from the stems, leaving them bare at the point where they are to be tied, as trapped leaves may go mouldy and rot.

Group the flowers in several bunches, staggering the levels of the heads. Use an elastic band rather than string or twine to hold the flowers as the flower stems shrink as they dry and the elastic will contract with the plant material. Form an 'S' shape hook with a stub wire and hook to the elastic band and use the other end to hang the bunch. Spread out the flowers and leaves to ensure the air can circulate and suspend the bunches from hooks, or an indoor clothes line.

To prevent the heads of heavy-headed flowers, such as roses, from drooping, wire the stems underneath the flowerheads before drying and group into bunches of about ten stems. Tie the stems together securely towards their ends and ease the wired stems outwards gently so that none of the flowerheads touchs. Once dry,

supporting wire stems can be disguised with green gutta-percha tape.

Any flowers that have heavy heads, such as onion flowers, should be dried individually with the heads supported by a wire rack.

DRYING FLAT

Grasses and seedheads that are supported on slender stems should be dried flat. Most mosses, bamboos, fungi and twigs also can be dried by this process. Although leaves keep their colour well by this method, they also tend to shrivel.

Lay a single layer of the plant material on an absorbent surface. Space out the material so the air can circulate. Turn the stems over occasionally to ensure that they dry out evenly.

STANDING – WET OR DRY

The best method to dry small, fragile flowers such as yarrow, fennel and dainty grasses is by inserting their stems into dry florist's foam.

Paradoxically, some flowers dry most successfully if they are left standing in water; this is the best way of preserving the colour and shape of hydrangea flowerheads, small peonies, and pom-pom dahlias. Stand the stems in 2.5-5cm (1-2in) of water and leave for two to three weeks. As the water evaporates, the plant material eventually dries out.

DRYING SEEDHEADS

It is important to pick seedheads for drying when they are fully formed but still green, just after the flower petals have fallen. Most seedheads can be dried using the basic hanging procedure, but some have special drying requirements. All the basic methods you need to know on air-drying are fully described step-by-step overleaf.

MOISTURE TESTS

If you are not sure that your flowers are completely dry, try these simple tests.
- Always test that a flower is dry in more than one place. Often the petals dry before the flower centre.
- Place a suspect flower or a few leaves in a small air-tight jar. Leave for a day or two. If condensation appears, the flowers and foliage need to be dried a little more.
- Often the 'neck' of the flower dries out last. Check that a bunch is dry by standing a sample flower upright in a container for 24-48 hours. The flowerhead will droop if the plant is not completely dry.

SUITABLE MATERIALS FOR AIR DRYING

1 Thick woody-stemmed plants with tiny flowers, such as golden rod (solidago), are particularly suitable for air drying. Detach any damaged flowerheads or imperfect upper leaves. Remove the lower foliage from the stems as they tend to retain moisture that may impede the drying process and cause the plant stem to rot.

5 This method involves wiring the flowerheads before drying them and is suited to heavy-headed blooms, such as roses, where the dried stems may be unable to support the weight of the flowerhead. Select good quality, undamaged flowers. Using a pair of scissors remove all the thorns and leaves from the stems.

acanthus	*dock*	*molucella*
achillea (yarrow)	*globe thistle*	*nigella*
African daisy	*golden rod*	*poppy*
allium	*gypsophila*	*sea holly*
anaphalis	*heather*	*shepherd's purse*
antirrhinum	*hollyhock*	*tansy*
astilbe	*hydrangea*	*teasel*
bluebell	*iris*	*thistle*
Chinese lantern	*lady's mantle*	*thrift*
clary	*larkspur*	
cornflower	*lavender*	
delphinium	*mimosa*	

2 Group the stems into bunches of four. Secure with an elastic band about 5cm (2 in) from the stem ends. Bind the ends with a piece of garden twine, leaving its ends free so that you can attach to a pole for drying. Dry right-way up following a few days hanging upside-down to counteract the natural drooping.

3 Repeat the same basic method for hollow-stemmed plants such as larkspur. Trim any excess greenery from the stems of one bunch of larkspur, as before, to guard against mould. Cut the flower stems to a length of 20cm (8 in). Group the flowers into bunches of four to five stems. If any of the stems appear weak, wire it for extra strength.

4 Secure with an elastic band. Spread out the stems so that they don't touch one another. Bend a length of thick gauge stub wire into an 'S' shape. Attach one end of this hook to the elastic band and use the other to hang the bunch.

6 Wire up each flower stem to hold the flowerheads in position. Use a 20cm (8 in) medium gauge stub wire to pierce the calyx, push the wire through the flower base and bend it over 2.5cm (1 in) from the top to form a 'U' shape. Pull this back into the calyx. Wind the wire once under the flowerhead and wrap the rest of the wire loosely around the stem.

7 Bunch the roses together. Large, full flowerheads, such as rose blooms, should not touch during the drying process, so arrange the heads so that they are on different levels. If the flowers are not staggered, the air will not be able to circulate freely around them and they could rot. Secure the stem ends together with an elastic band.

8 Make an 'S' shape from a thick gauge stub wire and attach this to the elastic band securing the roses. Erect a bamboo pole or a washing line in a cool, well-ventilated place and attach the roses to it. If you are hanging several bunches at one time, make sure that they do not touch. Leave the material until it is completely dry before arranging.

Drying with Desiccants

DESICCATED FLOWERS RETAIN ALL THE FRAGILE BEAUTY AND TONE OF FRESH FLOWERS YET WILL
LAST INDEFINITELY. USE THEM TO CREATE A PERMANENT BEDROOM DISPLAY.

Delicate fresh flowers can be preserved for arranging more successfully using desiccants than by air drying techniques examined in the previous pages, which are most suitable for everlasting flowers. Desiccants, such as silica crystals, alum, borax or sand, absorb moisture from the plant material and so preserve it. At its best, this method produces strikingly life-like blooms. However, the process is unpredictable and desiccated flowers are more likely to absorb atmospheric moisture than air-dried blooms.

Flowers dried using desiccants retain their colour well because the drying process is fast. However, this speed also means that the flowers may become rather brittle if they are left in the desiccant for too long.

It is best to dry short-stemmed flowers with desiccants as flowers with long stems tend to collapse before they are dry. In addition, the length of container and amount of desiccant required to dry long-stemmed material successfully can prove prohibitive in terms of expense.

Desiccants used for drying flowers must be in powder or small crystal form to prevent crushing fragile blooms. To achieve the most brilliantly colourful results for successful flower arranging, always ensure the flowers you choose to preserve are at their best. If picking from the garden, make sure the flowers are undamaged by insects or the weather. Also ensure that you pick them on a dry day either in the morning as described in the previous pages or, alternatively, pick them shortly before the evening dew has begun to form. If you have no access to a garden, visit your most reliable local florist and select the best flowers from there.

SILICA CRYSTALS

Silica crystals are the most popular of the four main types of desiccant. They are effective, quick – the process takes from two to five days depending on the size of the flower – and easy to use. Available from chemists, they come either as white crystals or with an added colour indicator which discloses any variations in the moisture content. The instructions on the packet will give details on the colour changes for particular crystals.

Although silica crystals are relatively expensive to buy, they can be used time and time again if you dry them between desiccating sessions. Spread out the moist, used crystals in an even layer on a baking tray and place in a cool oven until they have returned to their original colour. When dry, sift the crystals in a coarse mesh sieve to remove small pieces of plant material. Between drying flowers, store the crystals in an air-tight container.

Use fine crystals that are about the same size as sugar for all but the most robust of flowers. If you cannot obtain very fine desiccant, place larger crystals in a plastic bag and crush them with a rolling pin or grind them in a blender. Make sure that you clean your kitchen equipment very thoroughly afterwards to remove all traces of the desiccant.

ALUM AND BORAX

Alum and borax are less expensive than silica crystals and also can be purchased from chemists. Both are particularly effective for delicate petals, although occasionally they stick to the dried plant material and are difficult to remove. The drying process is similar to that for silica crystals, although it can take slightly longer – between seven to ten days. It is important to remember that alum and borax need to be sieved before use as the desiccant grains tend to clump together.

SAND

Before the introduction of chemical desiccants, sand was employed as a natural drying agent. Today, it is useful for drying large single flowerheads or several blooms at a time. Fine silver sand, available from garden centres, is the best sand to use as it has small, free-flowing grains that are cleaner than other types which must be washed and dried carefully before they can be used. Like alum and borax, sand takes between seven to ten days to absorb moisture from flowers.

Often silver sand is mixed with alum and borax in the ratio two parts sand to three parts chemical desiccant. To reuse, dry out in a warm oven.

USING DESICCANTS

Cut the flower stems to 2.5cm (1 in) long and wire the heads to make an artificial stem. Ease a short length of fine stub wire up through the stem and into the centre of the flower. Bend the tip of the wire into a 'U' shape and pull it back gently into the flower to secure it. To retain long flower stems for blooms such as hyacinths, insert a stub wire up through the full length of the stem to provide additional support for the fragile flowerhead.

Lay the flowerheads on a layer of desiccant, 2.5cm (1 in) deep in an airtight container such as a plastic freezer box, making sure that the plant material does not touch. Round faced flowers, such as pansies and buttercups, should be placed with their heads face down on a layer of desiccant. For larger, multi-petalled blooms, it helps to lay a wire mesh over the silica crystals and place the flowers in the mesh so that their heads are supported and the stems point down. Flower spikes, such as those of hollyhocks, should be placed on their sides.

DRYING FLOWERS IN DESICCANTS

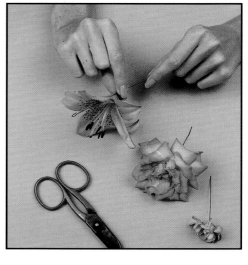

1 Select flowers. Cut the rose stem to a length of about 2.5cm (1 in) and trim a stub wire to 5cm (2 in). Ease one end of the wire into the calyx and wrap the rest around the remaining stem. Cut the lily stem to a length of 2.5cm (1 in) and insert a short length of wire through the stem base. Trim a single floret from the stock spire and wire in the same way as the lily.

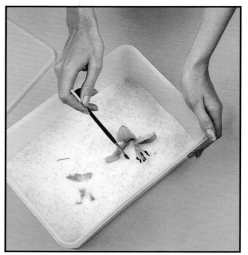

4 Use a very fine paintbrush to arrange the crystals around delicate flowerheads. To dry successfully, the flowerheads should be covered completely. Flowers can be placed at different levels throughout the desiccant, but ensure that the sturdier blooms are positioned at the bottom of the container.

INGREDIENTS

1 rose
2 stock
3 lily
4 dry silica crystals

5 deep plastic air-tight container
6 fine paint brush
7 fine gauge stub wires
8 scissors
9 measuring jug

2 Place a 2.5cm (1 in) layer of silica crystals in deep plastic air-tight container. Place the stock flowerhead downards in the crystals and position the larger flowerheads on their sides facing upwards on top of the layer of desiccant. Make sure that the flowers are well spaced and do not touch each other.

3 Using a measuring jug filled with silica crystals, pour the desiccant gently into the container and over the flowerheads. Continue adding crystals until the flowerheads are almost completely covered. If you are working with very fragile flowers, use your fingertips to sprinkle the desiccant carefully over the flowerheads.

Sift more desiccant gently around the flowers then run it carefully through your fingers so that it trickles between the petals and fills the crevices of the flower, right through to the centre. If necessary, use a small, fine paintbrush to ease the crystals into position. Make sure that you cover the whole of the flower.

DRYING TRUMPET-SHAPED FLOWERS

Trumpet-shaped flowerheads, or blooms with deep cups, should be filled with desiccant before being covered. Support the flower in your hand and fill it carefully with desiccant, then lower it gently into a desiccant-lined container and cover.

After a few days, brush away the top layer of desiccant gently from one flower. If the petals feel papery, carefully pour off the desiccant from the container, allowing the petals and flowers to fall into your hand. Brush away any remaining desiccant with the tip of a fine paintbrush. Any petals that have become detached can become re-attached using a clear adhesive applied with the point of a fine wooden cocktail stick. When not in use, store the delicate dried flowers on crumpled tissue paper in an air-tight container.

The following flower types are suitable for drying with desiccants:

anemone, buttercup, calendula, cornflower, daffodil, dahlia, daisy, delphinium, forget-me-not, geranium, bellebore, hollyhock, hyacinth, lily, lily of the valley, marigold, molucella, monkshood, paeony, pansy, primrose, rose, rudbeckia, stock, viola, violet.

5 Seal the lid of the container and store in a warm, dry place out of direct sunlight. The drying period will vary from between two to ten days, depending on the desiccant and the type of the flowers you use. If you are unsure your container is air-tight, use tape to seal the edges. Shake the container gently periodically to get rid of any air pockets.

6 The flowerheads are ready when they feel papery and dry to the touch. When the flowers are completely dry, tip out most of the crystals into their original container so that they can be dried and re-used. Lift the florets out of the desiccant and dust off the remainder of the crystals with a brush. Extend the wire stems ready for arranging.

STORING DESICCANT-DRIED FLOWERS

As already noted, flowers which have been dried in desiccants are especially brittle, and can be prone to reabsorption of moisture. To keep them in perfect condition, therefore, it is important to pay particular attention to the way they are stored.

Small flowers may be stored on crumpled tissue paper, in airtight containers. Large flowers, dahlias for example, may be stored with their stems held in a block of dry foam, in a dry room, away from strong light. For more details on storing, see pages 114 and 115.

Dried Flower Care

Whether you grow or collect your own flowers, seed pods and foliage for drying, or buy them ready dried, chances are, sooner or later, you'll have more than you need. Even if you don't have a specific project in mind, it's worth keeping them for future use. Properly packed and stored, they retain their colour and shape almost indefinitely, and if you make a regular habit of storing 'left-overs', however modest, you'll soon have quite a large reserve collection from which to create new displays.

Store the material somewhere airy, evenly warm, dust free and out of direct sunlight. (Keep flowers preserved in desiccant in airtight containers with a few silica gel crystals, though, since they are very vulnerable to the slightest atmospheric moisture.) Spare bedrooms and lofts are fine; sheds, garages and cellars can be damp in winter.

Always store material loosely, since tightly interlocked flowers are impossible to separate without breakage. Most dried material can be stored horizontally, in long cardboard boxes. Ask your florist for empty flower-delivery boxes, most of which have holes for ventilation; if not, you can easily make them. Loosely bunch flowers, foliage or seed pods, keeping species separate. Pack the bunches in layers, again keeping each type separate, and loosely overlapping them, head-to-toe, to use space efficiently. You can wrap each bunch in tissue paper first, for extra protection.

Store long flower spikes, such as larkspur, acanthus, or foxglove seedheads, individually, not bunched. Store flat material, such as dried ferns and grasses or glycerined beech, in flat layers, not bunched, with tissue paper between each layer. Always label boxes with the contents and date stored, and if you use some flowers more often than others, try to layer these at the top. Always include a few sprigs of dried artemisia or mothballs in the flower's storage containers, to discourage insects.

Dried material can also be stored hung upside down in loose bunches, ideally with a newspaper cone over each bunch, to protect it from light and dust. You can also store strong-stemmed material right-way up, in wide-mouthed coffee jars or cardboard boxes. Again, rest a single sheet of newspaper on top, to keep out any dust and light, unless you're displaying them decoratively, at the same time. Always store glycerined material on its own, since it sometimes oozes glycerine.

If you have room, you can insert large, individual flowers into blocks of florist's foam, or rest them on crumpled tissue paper, and store in hat boxes or shoe boxes, under a bed or in a spare closet.

From time to time, go through your stored material, throwing away anything damaged beyond repair and putting to one side faded material, for spraying silver or gold at Christmas-time. Any dull-looking glycerined leaves can be wiped with a tiny dab of vegetable oil before use, to bring back the shine.

Unused dried flowers, foliage, grasses and seedheads will spoil quickly if not stored properly. You may think that you never have enough excess arranging material to worry about special facilities for storing, but if you make dried-flower displays regularly, the leftovers soon pile up. Careful packing now will save you money in the future.

Most dried flowers and foliage are sold by the bunch. If you are making a small display, or an arrangement that requires a

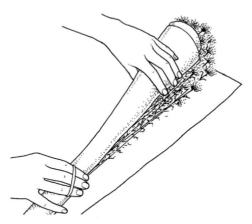

1 Storing delicate bunches
To store a bunch of delicate dried flowers, such as rhodanthe or roses, you should always use copious amounts of tissue paper. This will ensure that the delicate flowerheads are protected when they are stored in a box. Roll a sheet of tissue paper around the flowers you wish to store. Form the paper into a cone shape and gently secure with sticky tape. Pack the bunches loosely in a

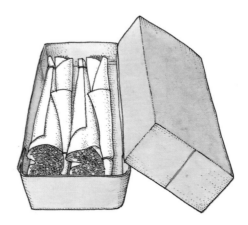

box, large enough to accommodate them without crushing them. To reduce risk of the flowers crumbling, make sure that you pack the wrapped bunches with the flowerheads lying in opposite directions.

variety of flowers but only a few stems of each flower type, about half a bunch of each will be left over. This material needs careful storage if it is to be usable at a later date. In addition, it is often the case that material can be salvaged when you take apart an old arrangement and put its ingredients to one side for re-use later.

Equally, if you dry your own material, you probably dry more than you can arrange all in one go and so you will need somewhere to store the excess.

WASTE NOT . . . . .
Almost as soon as you have completed your first dried flower arrangement, you will realise that every component, however small or seemingly insignificant, can have a decorative part to play in a future design. And so, in this context, the maxim is, don't throw anything away.

If strawflowers (helichrysum) flowerheads break away from their stalks in storage, as you are arranging them, store them in a single layer in a box until you have time to mount them on false stems such as stub wires, as shown on page 120.

The daisy-like flowers have other applications, too. You can stick them on an old picture frame or the rim of a basket, especially one that is to be filled with pot pourri.

Side shoots that, for design reasons, have to be cut from the stems of large-scale flowers and foliage, such as larkspur, delphinium and eucalyptus, can be stored separately and used in small or even miniature arrangements. Ears of dried wheat or corn which have become detached from their brittle stems can be positioned to form a ring around a candle in a country-style design. And the hollow stems have potential too. You can use them to make realistic false stems for a variety of flowers which have become detached from their natural stems – ones which have been cut before desiccant drying, for example.

STORAGE GUIDE
Different types of material require different methods of storage according to shape, size and fragility. The four steps below illustrate the best ways of storing particular flower types.

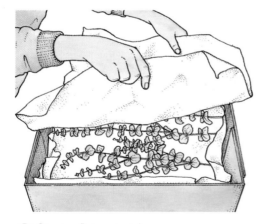

2 Storing flat material
To pack flat sprays of material, such as dried eucalyptus, or ferns, fill the bottom of a cardboard box with crumpled tissue paper. Place the material in a single layer. Add another layer of tissue paper and a layer of plant material on to. Fill to within 2.5cm (1 in) of top of the box. Place a single piece of tissue paper on top and cover.

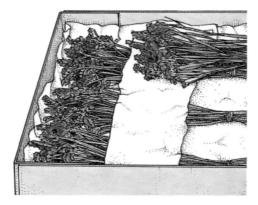

3 Storing flower bunches
Bind the dried flowers, such as statice or larkspur, into small bunches with string. Lie them side by side at one end of a large box. Cover ends of stems with tissue paper. Build up the second row by placing bunches on top of tissue paper covering stems of the row below, so that just the flowerheads are visible. Finish off with a layer of tissue paper and cover.

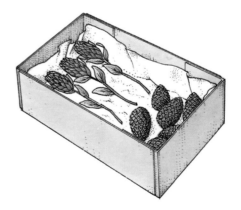

4 Storing bulky items
Fill a large basket or box with plenty of crumpled tissue paper. Place large, bulky or fragile material such as seedheads, cones or moss carefully in separate parts of the tissue paper 'nest'. Place a final layer of crumpled paper on top and cover the box or basket with a lid. Use this form of safe storage to pack away complete small arrangements.

Dried Flower Spectrum

BRIGHT CHEERFUL DRIED FLOWERS COMBINE IN AN ORIGINAL DISPLAY INSPIRED BY THE SPECTRUM,
SET IN A ROUGHLY WOVEN RUSTIC BASKET

The majority of flower arrangements, whether dried or fresh, combine several different coloured materials to achieve an integrated effect. Sometimes this involves adjusting one or two flowers in a finished display so that adjacent areas of colour are blended to achieve a well-balanced effect. In other designs, small areas of many different colours are blended together to achieve a tapestry effect, rather like the look of a field of mixed wild flowers. In this project, however, flower colour is used differently; the various dried materials are kept apart deliberately to form blocks of contrasting colour, for a refreshing, new, modern-looking design.

FORM AND TEXTURE

It is usually advisable to avoid using dyed plant material in a dried flower arrangement since their uniform intensity can 'kill' the subtle colour variation of natural material. For this project, however, dyed flowers are an asset, since they help to emphasise the distinct colour sections. Often, dried-flower suppliers colour different species using the same dye to achieve perfect colour co-ordination in displays. Take advantage of this when you are selecting your ingredients and choose ready colour-matched flowers that have contrasting shapes.

The form and texture of the individual flowers play an important role in this display. However, these differences are subtle and do not extend to contrasts in size. Sizes range from the lace-like broom bloom to medium-sized love-in-a-mist seed pods, but nothing larger or bolder is included. As the materials are bunched together before they are arranged, individually dramatic blooms would detract from the overall design.

CHOOSING THE MATERIAL

All the plant materials featured here are available from florist shops that stock dried flowers. Alternatively, visit a garden centre, department store with a dried-flower section or a specialist dried flower shop. Such places often have stands full of dried material, arranged according to colour, which should help you make your selection. Always hold up bunches of flowers next to each other and try out possible colour combinations before making your final choice.

VARIOUS HUES

The yellow section is made up of dried achillea, buttercups and lady's mantle in their natural colours, and dyed yellow anaphalis. Natural-coloured alternatives include yellow kangaroo paw, annual sea lavender, golden morrison, verticordia or any of the yellow, cluster-flowered helichrysums. If you prefer yellow-dyed materials, try using bright-yellow dyed lagurus, or hare's-tail grass, yellow-dyed gypsophila, perennial sea lavender, broom bloom or lesser or greater quaking grass.

VARY THE HUES

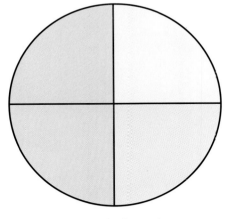 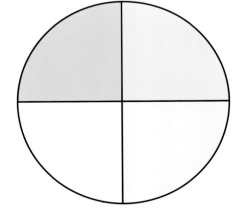

1 As an alternative to the featured arrangement using blocks of contrasting or complementary colour, make a soothing display of harmonizing flowers by combining colours that are adjacent or close to each other on the colour wheel. For example, use pink helichrysum, violet delpinium, blue-violet statice and blue cornflowers.

2 Single colour displays are more subtle than complementary or harmonising arrangements. They rely on minor variations of colour to be effective. Team flowers in shades of the same colour in a container of a matching hue. For example, for a colour combination that features colours graduating from pale yellow to rich gold, combine pale yellow helichrysum, lady's mantle, yarrow and mimosa.

The reds and pinks are represented by roses, dyed broom bloom, dyed phalaris and dyed anaphalis. Again, a few pink helichrysums could be substituted or pink annual statice. An unusual alternative is red, velvety cockscomb, broken into small sections and wired separately. It has an intricately folded structure which would add textural interest to this arrangement. There are relatively few dried, naturally blue flowers. Larkspur is the most widely available but is unsuitable for inclusion in this display as its spiky form is out of keeping with the other materials. Luckily

there are many blue-dyed flowers from which to choose. Here, pale-blue-dyed and deep-blue-dyed briza and blue-dyed camomile are used, but you could substitute blue-dyed stirlingia, ti-tree, helipterum or broom bloom. Lavender is blue-mauve, and its tiny spikes would add textural interest to this arrangement; small poppy seedheads, left in their natural pale colour, appear blue when grouped with other blue plant material.

The central feature in this display is a bunch of small-flowered white achillea; white gypsophila or dill would be fine

or bleached lagurus, broom bloom or immortelle.

Lastly, green love-in-a-mist seed pods add bulk to a more subtly coloured group of pale pinks and greens. You could replace these with unopened carthamus flower buds if preferred.

CHOOSING THE CONTAINER
The featured display is created in an old-fashioned style, woven wicker basket, 30cm (12 in) in diameter. A larger or smaller basket, a bleached wicker basket or a basket with a handle also would be

MAKING A VIVID BASKET
DISPLAY OF DRIED FLOWERS

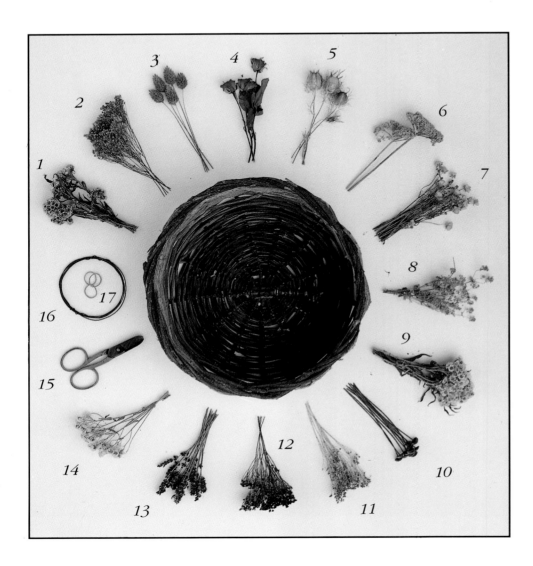

1 Cut a length of gardening wire to at least twice the diameter of the basket. Push one end through the basket weave. Pull it taut over to the other side of the basket and hook it through the weave. Pull it back to the side you started on and twist it through the basket weave to secure. Repeat with another length of wire at right angles to the first, dividing the basket into four segments.

4 Make up the blue posy. Make the bulk of the posy with two bunches of pale and dark blue briza. Insert small bunches of blue-dyed camomile to add textural interest. Place one bunch of lavender in the middle. Bind the stems with an elastic band. Trim the stems ends to equal length. Place in the basket beside the red bunch and opposite the yellow.

INGREDIENTS

1 1 bunch of pink-dyed anaphalis
2 2 bunches of pink-dyed briza
3 1 bunch of pink-dyed phalaris
4 10 stems of red rose-buds
5 1 bunch of love-in-a-mist
6 4 stems of large achillea
7 4 bunches of buttercups
8 1 bunch of lady's mantle
9 2 bunches of yellow anaphalis

10 2 bunches of blue-dyed camomile
11 1 bunch of pale-blue briza
12 1 bunch of dark-blue briza
13 1 bunch of lavender
14 1 bunch of achillea
15 scissors
16 gardening wires
17 elastic bands
18 basket

2 Make up a posy of the pink flowers. Build up the basic shape of the posy with two bunches of pink-dyed anaphalis. Place four red rose-buds in the centre. Frame the anaphalis with stems of phalaris. Bind the posy with an elastic band to hold the stems loosely together. Trim the stems to equal lengths. Place the posy in one of the wired-off sections.

3 Make up a similar-sized posy using two bunches of yellow anaphalis, four stems of large achillea and four bunches of buttercups. Form the centre of the posy using the anaphalis and frame this with the buttercups. Insert four large achillea heads in the centre. Bind the stems with an elastic band and trim the stems. Place in one of the sections beside the pink bunch.

suitable. Alternatively, try one of the baskets available with moss interwoven with the wicker.

A round, wooden bread basket or salad bowl makes an interesting alternative, and you could construct smaller, subsidiary displays of single-colour, dried-flower posies in individual salad bowls and group them in a circle round the main bowl. This would make a particularly interesting table centre-piece.

If you wish to use a square or broadly rectangular basket, divide it into four smaller squares or rectangles to achieve even blocks of colour.

USING NON-WOVEN CONTAINERS

You also could create a display in a plain china bowl but avoid heavily decorated ones that may detract from the theme of the arrangement. If you are using a glass bowl, line it first with dried sphagnum moss or raffia ribbon – opened out and wrapped in a circle round the inside – so that the flower stems are not visible.

If using a non-woven container, use a single layer of large-mesh, crumpled chicken-wire netting, slightly wider than the diameter of the container, as a stem-supporting foundation.

CHOOSING THE SETTING

The basket is shown on a stripped pine, country-kitchen table, but it would suit a formica-topped, glass-topped or polished, dark wood table equally well. Alternatively, you could buy a length of inexpensive cotton fabric in colours matching the flowers and hem or fringe it to make a cheerful, colour co-ordinated table-cloth. Take this idea one stage further and pick out the various colour blocks in the shades of matching napkins.

5 For the last section, choose a more muted colour selection in pale pinks and green. Make the bulk of the posy from pink-dyed briza. Surround the briza with a ring of love-in-a-mist and place four red roses in the centre. Fill out the posy with lady's mantle. Bind the stems with a rubber band. Trim the stems. Insert into the section in the basket.

6 Finally, to add colour contrast in the centre of the arrangement, make up a small bunch of white achillea. Trim the stems. Place in the centre of the display so that the bunch sits slightly higher than the other materials. Tease open all the bunches to fill out each section of the basket, disguise the wires to give a full, brimming effect.

With its concentration of bright, cheerful colours this design would look equally at home on a small hearth, where it would add visual warmth to any room, and where the mass of flowers would be seen to advantage from above. If the size is right, you could place the basket actually in the fire grate. In this case, it would be best to tilt the flower basket slightly forwards, so that the rainbow colour effect can be fully appreciated.

Modern Dried Display

TEAM THE BRIGHTEST DRIED FLOWERS WITH A MODERN CERAMIC BOWL TO BRING VITALITY TO A
CONTEMPORARY SETTING

This modern dried flower display should give you the inspiration to be adventurous and experiment with colour in ways that you might previously have thought were only possible when using fresh flowers. Although the shades of flower are bold, the round posy design is one of the simplest to construct, and therefore you only need worry about getting the colours right.

The colour theme for your arrangement should be suggested by the container. Choose the brightest bowl you can find, and dare to be brash in matching the flowers you use to the colours of the container.

VIBRANT AND RESTFUL SHADES
Dark-blue larkspur, pink rhodanthe, deep-purple statice and pure-yellow helichrysum are used here in roughly equal proportions; each colour is bright and clear, and chosen to complement the container. Purple and yellow are opposites on the colour wheel and are therefore most vibrant when put next to each other.

Part of the reason that this featured display is so eye-catching is the extremes in contrast within the flower colours. If you want the intense colour contrast shown, avoid white or subtle colours.

CHOOSING THE FLOWERS AND FOLIAGE
All the flowers used are commercially grown and should be widely available. If you do make substitutions, try to get a good mixture of spiky and rounded flowers, to break up the outline of the display.

One large bunch of dark-blue larkspur is used for this display. Larkspur is a hardy annual. As an alternative to the dark-blue larkspur, you could use dark-blue monkshood, or blue-purple astilbe.

One large bunch of pink rhodanthe, or Swan River everlasting, is used in this display. Australian in origin, rhodanthe's, wiry stems are usually too weak to insert into florist's foam blocks, so the flowers are wired up, either individually (see box), or in bunches of 6-12 flowers. Instead of rhodanthe, you could use the clover-like pink globe amaranths.

One bunch of yellow helichrysum, or strawflower, is included in the arrangement featured here. You may have to order an all-yellow bunch in advance from your florist. Helichrysum is another annual everlasting flower. In this display, the strawflowers, with their flat disc-shaped blossom, provide the largest mass of colour so remember, whatever colour strawflower you use, it will carry extra visual weight. Purple statice, or sea lavender, provides a lace-like touch.

The dried foliage featured here is blue leaf, an Australian species of acacia. It is related to florist's mimosa. Instead of blue leaf, you could use a small-leafed variety of eucalyptus, but avoid large-leafed eucalyptus, as this would not lend itself to building up a dense mass of material.

CHOOSING THE CONTAINER
The container shown here is a hand-

WIRING BROKEN FLOWERHEADS

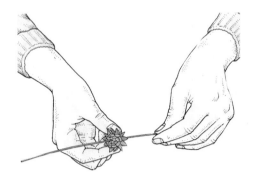

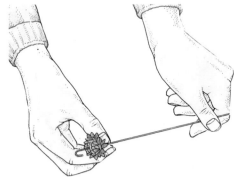

Should any of the helichrysum flowerheads break off while you are inserting them into an arrangement, do not throw them away – wire them instead. They can be used as infill flowers in tightly-packed displays. This a different technique from wiring groups of flowerheads.

1 Push a piece of medium-gauge stub wire up through the centre of the flowerhead at the point where the stem used to be.

2 Make a small hook in the top of the wire by bending over the wire by bending over the wire 2.5cm (1 in) from the end, and pull the wire gently down until it catches in the middle of the flower.

MAKING A MODERN DISPLAY

1 Prepare the foam by pressing the block onto the rim of the bowl and using the imprint as a template. Shave off the excess foam, angling your cuts inward so that the block follows the contours of the bowl. Make sure that 2.5cm (1 in) of the foam sits above the rim of the bowl. Secure the foam with two lengths of florist's adhesive tape.

4 Break off the yellow helichrysum stems into lengths, 7.5-10cm (3-4 in) long. Position the helichrysum heads just below the level of the blue leaf and the larkspur to avoid a smooth ball effect. If any of the heads should break off while you are working, wire them onto false stems (see box). Angle the stems of the bottom gently downwards.

INGREDIENTS

1 *large bunch of blue larkspur*
2 *large bunch of pink rhodanthe*
3 *small bunch of blue leaf*
4 *large bunch of purple statice*
5 *large bunch of yellow helichrysum*

6 *bright pottery bowl*
7 *knife*
8 *scissors*
9 *florist's adhesive tape*
10 *block of dry florist's foam*

2 Divide each stem of blue leaf into three lengths of about 10-13cm (4-5 in). Strip the foliage from the bottom of each stem and push into the foam. Place a single stem in the centre of the block to set the height, and insert the other stems at an angle at intervals to cover the foam block. Angle the stems around the rim slightly downwards.

3 Using the whole stem, divide the blue larkspur into lengths of about 7.5-10cm (3-4 in). Position the larkspur at an angle in between the blue leaf to build up a domed look. Vary the length of the stems in order to avoid an unnaturally smooth effect. Cover the whole of the foam block, but ensure that the flowers have been placed evenly throughout.

5 Group the pink rhodanthe into clusters of about three to four stems and cut 5-7.5cm (2-3 in) from the heads. Graduate the heads within the cluster. Hold the stems close to the end and ease them into the foam. If the flowers are very weak, wire them into florets. Intersperse the clusters throughout the arrangement.

6 Break off the statice stems 5-7.5cm (2-3 in) from the head. Use the statice to fill any gaps in the display and ensure that the foam block is completely covered. Vary the lengths of the stems to achieve a natural-looking result. Turn the bowl as you work and study the arrangement from above to ensure the flowers are evenly distributed.

painted, glazed ceramic bowl, with semi-abstract patterns in blue, green, yellow and pink. Choose an informal, modern, bright bowl and match the flowers to the colours of the pattern. The kind of pottery available cheaply in many Mediterranean countries is ideal.

You could also use a single-coloured container and repeat this in one of the flower colours; bright yellow would be especially arresting.

Another interesting idea is to choose a blue and white Chinese bowl of the kind readily available in kitchen equipment shops. Whether it is decorated with a characteristic flower and leaf design, with an abstract pattern, or geometric shapes, an Oriental bowl would harmonize with the sharp yellow and muted pink colour scheme in the featured display. For an even more eye-catching combination in a blue-and-white container, you could team strawflowers (helichrysum), in bright yellow – a traditional colour in Chinese floral art – with deep blue larkspur, blue and white statice, and white rhodanthe.

CHOOSING THE SETTING

This round display makes a perfect table centrepiece for a dinner party, or a low table in the living room. The featured setting is ultra-modern, and the stark black and white background and modern furnishing points up the dynamic colours of the flowers. If you have a more traditional decor, the display would look equally good situated in a neutural interior: pine, white or pale walls, and neutral carpets and furnishing fabrics. To keep the flower colours vivid for as long as possible choose a location which is out of direct sunlight as strong light fades flowers.

In fact, this brightly-coloured display does not need strong light of any kind to enhance its charm. On the contrary, it could be placed to good effect in a dark corner, in an alcove, or on a bookshelf, where it would seem to bring a warm glow to that part of the room. This is because the arrangement includes both strawflowers (helichrysum) and rhodanthe everlasting flowers which, unlike so many dried flowers are composed of shiny petals which reflect every shaft of available light and so give a visual 'lift' to the design.

Dried Flower Tree

DRIED-FLOWER TREES ARE THE LATEST FASHION AND, THOUGH EXPENSIVE TO BUY, ARE EASY AND
CHEAP TO MAKE AND WILL AUTOMATICALLY ADD A TOUCH OF CLASS TO ANY DECOR

Dried flower trees look impressive in any home. They look just right in a traditional setting but look equally good in a modern setting too. They come in many shapes and sizes; here we describe how to make a miniature dried flower tree. These pretty little trees are surprisingly easy – and great fun – to put together, even if you have never tried arranging with dried flowers before. Just make sure that you have all the necessary 'ingredients' to hand, then follow the easy to follow step-by-step instructions.

Your tree could be the focal point of the room, or a corner detail that provides the perfect 'finishing touch'. Either way, a dried-flower tree gives value for money and space, needs very little looking after and adds extra style to your home.

CHOOSING YOUR FLOWERS

First of all decide on the colour of your tree, taking into account the colour scheme in the room where the tree is to go, and whether you would like it to stand out boldly or blend discreetly into the background. Once you decided on the colour, choose your dried flowers from your local florist, or a shop that specialises in dried flowers. Many large department stores now also stock a wide selection.

If you cannot find all the other items needed for the tree at the florist's, try your local garden centre or a hardware shop. Plaster-of-Paris powder is available from your local DIY store (or preferably a superstore) where you are sure to be able to buy a 1kg (2 lb) bag – which is all you will need for the ball-tree base.

PREPARING YOUR TREE

The old-fashioned foundation for the head of the dried-flower ball tree is dried sphagnum moss packed into a rough globe shape, then encased in wire mesh netting. It is easier to use dried-flower foam balls, which range from 7.5cm (3 in) to 25cm (10 in) or more in diameter. For larger balls, you can use two or more blocks of foam packed together and roughly cut to form a globe shape, then held firmly with wire mesh netting.

Remember, though, that the finished ball can be much wider than the diameter

WIRING A BUNCH OF HELICHRYSUM

Helichrysum and other flowers are often wired in bunches for ball tree arrangements. By grouping them together in florets you can strengthen the colour in areas of your display.
1 Take four stems of flowers. Gather up the stems and cut them approximately 5cm (2 in) from their heads.

2 Take a 17.5cm (7 in) length of stub wire and bend a length back about 5cm (2 in) from the top. Place the shorter piece of wire against the stems of the flowers and begin to twist the longer length around the stems. Dried flowers are rather brittle, so be careful.

3 Twist the wire tightly around the stems at least three times to secure the stems together. Cut the long piece of wire to the required length, making sure that you have enough to press into the block of florist's foam so that the floret will stand up firmly in the arrangement.

FORMING A DRIED FLOWER TREE

1 Once the pot base is prepared (see box, right), insert the stick, and then spoon in more plaster-of-Paris to fill the pot to within 12mm (½ in) of the rim. When the stick is firmly held, wind a short length of adhesive clay around the top. Press the foam onto the stick. For this ball tree you need a stem about 38cm (14 in) high.

4 Wire together the flower stems into small groups (see box on wiring). You only need wire those with weaker stems, the everlastings, helichrysum, lavender and glixia. Bunch together three or four pieces of the other ingredients and insert them at random in groups into the foam.

INGREDIENTS

1 Statice dumosa
2 green amaranthus
3 bleached broom bloom
4 lavender
5 fresh moss
6 cream glixia
7 cream helichrysum
8 everlastings

9 eryngium
10 adhesive clay
11 pre-cut 17.5cm (7 in) stub wires
12 38cm (14 in) stick
13 floristry scissors
14 1kg (2 lb) of plaster-of-Paris

15 dry foam ball 12cm (5 in) in diameter
16 medium-sized terracotta pot
17 tape measure
18 roll of 5mm (¼ in) florist's tape

2 Secure the foam ball using 5mm adhesive tape. Wind the tape around the stick at the base and over the top of the foam. Wind the tape around the stick again and back over the ball at right angles to the previous tape. Following the tape line, insert small bunches of *Statice dumosa*, about 8cm (3 in) in length.

3 Continue adding small bunches of statice, filling in each quarter of the foam until it is evenly covered. Fill in any remaining gaps, turning the tree around so you are sure you have achieved a rounded shape. It is best to work on a table top so that you can look at the tree from above as well as from underneath.

5 Begin with any group and insert the ingredients firmly at a slight angle. Support the tree stem firmly in one hand and hold the wire at the base of the flowerheads in the other. Keep turning the tree to ensure you get an even cover and to avoid large patches of colour. The fuller this arrangement is, the better.

6 Cover the tree base and the plaster in the pot with a layer of fresh moss. Press down firmly. For a more permanent finish, glue the moss to the base with transparent glue. Give your tree one last turn, to check you have a full, rounded shape. Don't trim your tree into an exact sphere or the result will be too rigid.

of the foundation, so you are unlikely to need a huge lump of foam. It is better in any case to have a smaller, but fully covered tree that is really attractive, than a huge, sparse, bald one.

Some people use polystyrene balls, but these are difficult to stick stems into and are more suitable for glued on flower-heads such as helichrysum. The trunk should be strong enough to support the flowers, but not heavy looking. As well as wooden dowels, broom handles, and natural wooden stems or branches, including the woody stems of such herbaceous plants as gypsophila, dahlia and cow parsley, you could use stainless steel or plastic rods for a modern tree. When considering the length, remember that for maximum stability, the trunk has to be inserted deeply into the container and the ball.

Heavy containers are safest, obviously you don't want your work of art to topple over. Use plaster-of-Paris, pebbles or even a brick to add weight to the container.

Traditional dried-flower trees, with poker-straight stems and perfect globes of evenly-packed flowers, have formal overtones. Such trees are ideal for more traditional settings, but dried flower trees can also be informal in feeling. Using a slightly curved tree branch and dried grasses or flexible-stemmed flowers to break the rigid, symmetrical outlines of the ball gives a relaxed, natural-looking effect. Informal dried-flower trees often have more character than the perfectly round trees which can sometimes look too bland and anonymous.

PREPARING THE BASE

Cut slivers of foam off the spare foam block and use them to line the terracotta pot. Put about 1 kg (2 lb) of plaster-of-Paris into a mixing bowl (you may need a little more or a little less, depending on the size of your pot). Slowly add cold water, mixing the powder with a metal spoon as you go, until the consistency is creamy smooth. You must be ready to go on to Step 1 as soon as you have completed this stage. Spoon the mixture quickly into the pot, before it sets, until it is two thirds full.

VIBRANT COMBINATIONS

If the lemon and green colours of our featured dried-flower tree are not to your liking, or do not match your furnishings, it is relatively simple to pick alternative dried flowers to suit your needs. A wonderful range of dried material in a variety of matching and contrasting colours, shapes and textures are available in the shops. This detail of another tree illustrates a range of closely matching pink and pale green tones. Eight different dried flowers and foliage were used including green amaranthus, rich red everlastings, peonies, *Statice dumosa*, wheat and helipterum. Alternatively, you may want to break away from the country-style look and use vibrant colour combinations to create striking, new modern trees.

CHOOSING THE RIGHT CONTAINER

The container you choose also affects the finished look. Versailles tubs – the square wooden plant holders with a wooden ball at each corner – are definitely formal in feeling, while an ordinary terracotta flower pot or woven wicker basket is more casual-looking.

Always decide where your tree is to go before you start, and whether it is to be seen on all sides or from one side only. If it has a definite front, such as a tree displayed up against a wall, you might want to concentrate the most colourful flowers there, or make a focal point of an especially beautiful bloom or cluster of flowers.

CHOOSING THE SETTING

A row of small dried-flower trees can brighten up a shelf, the top of a bookcase, or the centre of a dining room table.

Miniature dried-flower trees would also be delightful as individual place setting decorations.

A dried-flower tree placed in front of a mirror is doubly impressive providing the back of the tree is as attractive as the front.

A pair of larger, dried-flower trees either side of the entrance to a room or disused fireplace would be impressive, and three or four large dried-flower trees would make an excellent room divider.

WATCHPOINTS

As well as the artistic aspects of deciding where your dried-flower tree should go, consider the practical ones.

Position dried-flower trees where they will be very safe from children, pets and accidental bumps. Weight floor-standing dried-flower tree containers, with stones or pebbles so that they can't be easily knocked over. Dried flowers are highly flammable, so keep them well away from open flames and other sources of heat. Stand your tree in a spot that is well out of direct sunlight, to prevent the flowers fading. Dried flowers are damaged by even tiny amounts of moisture in the air, so don't place a tree in a damp sun-porch for example, or outside.

ABOVE LEFT **The unusual knobbly, twisted trunk of this original little tree would make it an eye-catching feature in any location. The beauty of this design lies in its simplicity: only one type of flower has been used, in a sharp lemon-green tone to give the tree a sophisticated look.**

RIGHT **White and dark green statice form the background of this large floor-standing ball tree. Bright shades of pink helichrysum, from the palest to the most vibrant, combine to make an attractie feature in a dark hallway.**

Woodland Landscape

FOR DRAMA ON A GRAND SCALE, TRY THIS EXCITING FANTASY LANDSCAPE, INSPIRED BY THE
AUSTERE NATURAL BEAUTY OF A WINTER HEDGEROW

This is a project for a long, winter's afternoon or evening. It is time-consuming but not difficult – all you need is a good selection of dried materials, plenty of space and a sense of adventure. If you're short of time, you can build up the display in stages over several days, stopping at the end of any of the six steps, and continuing later.

The idea behind this type of arrangement, sometimes called a 'vegetative' display, is to recreate the spirit of plants growing in a landscape. The idea comes from a Japanese flower-arranging style, called Moribana, based on creating natural-looking landscapes, or 'memory sketches'. Inspiration for the style of the arrangement comes from nature.

NATURE IN MINIATURE
If you try to create a perfectly accurate scaled-down landscape, like miniature model train scenery, you will get caught up in details. Instead, try to capture the spirit of the idea: the silhouette of bare branches against the sky, the intricate collection of leaves, mosses and seed pods at the base of a hedgerow and the subdued palette of winter colours, brightened by touches of autumnal golds and bronzes.

Build the arrangement where you intend to display it, as moving a large, heavy, delicately-balanced display around is likely to cause damage. Don't be disappointed if you can't obtain every ingredient shown here. Availability of seedheads, seed pods, leaves and fungus varies from place to place, and season to season. However, if you have enough dried material to make a generously full display, and you follow the relaxed, informal approach, you should get good results.

CHOOSING THE INGREDIENTS
Dried red roses are the most prominent flowers used, and their strong colour adds a rich, wintery feel – pale pink or yellow ones would be too spring-like. Because their stems are cut short, you could use the cheaper dried 'sweetheart' roses. If you can only obtain long-stemmed roses, save the cut-off stems and foliage for use in other displays.

Dried mophead hydrangeas are as useful in an arrangement as gypsophila; both are excellent fillers, attractive in themselves yet they allow other, more sculptural or dramatic flowers, to attract the eye. Dried hydrangeas range in shade from russet-red to blue, green and, as used here, a neutral, papery beige.

Bleached broom bloom is available only from florists, and is as much valued for its delicate branches and stalks as for its tiny flowers. In this display, its pale colour stands out strongly against the deeper tones. For a more subtle effect, you could use russet or tan-dyed broom bloom as an alternative.

If you grow poppies, you can collect your own seed pods in autumn, and air-dry them until needed. Dried poppy seedheads are widely available, in natural pale silver-grey, as used here, or in a range of dyed colours.

DRYING AND VARNISHING GOURDS

To dry ornamental gourds, wash off soil with mild disinfectant, then pat dry and prick each end with a needle or dressmaker's pin. Place them somewhere warm to dry out. Inspect them after four to six weeks; if they feel light in relation to their size and you can hear the seeds rattle when you shake them, they're fully dry and ready to varnish. Glaze gourds with varnish to make their matt skin glossy and to make them last longer. This only works if the gourds are fully dried first, otherwise moisture will be trapped inside and they will rot.

BUYING DRIED SEEDHEADS
Chinese lanterns, like poppies, are traditional dried flowers, available from most large dried-flower suppliers. When you buy them, check that the orange lanterns – actually coloured calyces – are intact and not cracked or otherwise damaged. If they come prepackaged in cellophane and some have broken off, you can still make use of them by glueing them directly onto the foam block in your display.

Walnuts are available from any supermarket and from most fruit and vegetable shops. You can use brazil nuts or pecans instead, and varnish them to enhance the sheen on their shells.

The leaves shown here are commercially preserved, but home-pressed or glycerined leaves would add a personal touch. Dried leaves are more fragile than glycerined ones, so handle them with special care.

A medley of unusual and exotic seed pods is incorporated into the base, including lotus, eucalyptus, leucodendron protea bases and dried globe artichokes. Those not on their own stems are available pre-wired, for easy use, and the larger ones are often sold as pods, to add contrast and sculptural interest.

CHOOSING THE OTHER INGREDIENTS

The other main ingredients that are needed to make this display are listed here. Leafless branches form the main vertical element of the display, and represent trees. Here, birch branches are used, but you could use hazel, alder, willow or even colourful dogwood branches.

Your florist may be able to supply you with a lichen-covered larch stem. You could also use a lichen-covered branch from an old apple or plum tree.

Birch bark and thin cross-cuts of wood which are ideal for this arrangement, are easier to find if you live in the country, otherwise ask your florist.

You should buy ornamental gourds as early in autumn as possible, to get the best selection and to be able to fully dry them before use. Some florists do carry them

CREATING YOUR
LANDSCAPE DISPLAY

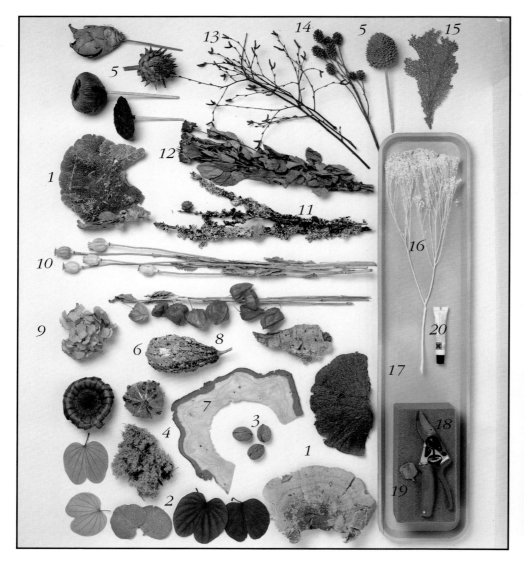

1 Attach three foam blocks onto a tray with prongs. Glue two bracket fungi onto the block, to overhang the edges: one in the back left corner, facing you, one in the back right corner. Push three bracket fungi into the front side of the block: in the centre, to the right, and in the right corner. Insert a birch branch, off centre, to set the height.

4 Insert leaves in horizontal rows of one colour each, under the bark and between the bracket fungi, to unify the display. Make a thicket of leucodendron in front of the tall branches. Fill in bare spots with shorter-stemmed seed pods such as lotus, artichoke and eucalyptus. Glue three clusters of two to three walnuts onto the bracket fungi.

INGREDIENTS

1 *3 large bracket fungi*
2 *20 assorted dried or glycerined leaves*
3 *8 walnuts*
4 *3 clumps of fresh reindeer moss*
5 *6 assorted exotic seedpods*
6 *5 gourds*
7 *3 thin wood crosscuts*
8 *10 Chinese lantern stems*
9 *1 hydrangea head*
10 *29 dried poppy seedheads*
11 *3 lichen-covered larch branches*
12 *15 dried red roses*
13 *4 birch branches*
14 *24 stems of leucodendron*
15 *1 piece of pink coral*
16 *12 bunches of white broom bloom*
17 *1 sprayed plastic plant tray*
18 *secateurs*
19 *3 prongs and florist's foam*
20 *quick-drying adhesive glue*

well into winter. You could use small edible gourds or squashes, although not all are suitable for drying and some go soft if they are stored in a warm room.

A few clumps of dried reindeer moss are used to camouflage the foam block base. Reindeer moss is a lichen, more closely related to the lichen on the larch branch than to green mosses.

Bracket fungi are also used to hide the base, and to add broad horizontal lines and sweeps of subtle colour.

Fan coral is available in various sizes from tropical fish shops specialising in marine fish. It is surprisingly inexpensive, and although a dusky pink piece is used here, you could also use white.

CHOOSING THE CONTAINER

An inexpensive plastic plant tray forms the base of this display. You can buy these from garden centres, and also garden departments of larger DIY centres.

Here, a white tray is used, but its glaring whiteness is softened by spraying it lightly with pale pink paint. You could spray it according to the colour scheme of the setting and your own taste.

You could use any plastic or metal serving tray you have, provided it's not too brightly coloured or heavily patterned. Remember that it is in use for as long as the display is intact.

As no water is needed, you could build the whole display on a rimless plank of wood – a rough-hewn piece of wavy-edged elm would be ideal to extend the woodland theme through the base. You can usually buy offcuts of softwoods, such as larch or pine, from timber yards and the larger do-it-yourself timber merchants.

You could use a wooden carving board, impaling the dried-flower florist's foam directly onto the meat spikes.

2 Insert four short birch branches around the main one, and a smaller cluster to the left. Lay clumps of reindeer moss on the foam, in the middle, and at each side. Break hydrangea heads into florets; insert round the front bracket fungi. Remove most of the leaves from ten Chinese lantern stems. Insert in a group in the middle. Add five gourds.

3 Shorten 15 rose stems; make the tallest about half the height of the short clump of branches, and the shortest, 7.5cm (3 in). Make a tight group of roses to your left, in front of the branches. Splay the roses out, to get a roughly oval outline. Insert the thin bark crosscuts into the sizes of the foam block, to extend the horizontal lines.

CHOOSING THE SETTING

The large size of this display precludes the usual settings such as bookshelves and dressing tables. If you have an old house with deep windowsills, place the display so sunlight filters through the 'trees'. Otherwise, the display needs a table to itself. If you are giving a post-Christmas winter buffet, it would make a fine centre-piece.

5 Rest a larch branch across the front, weaving it through nearby material. Insert two small branches in the sides of the block to extend the line. Build up a vertical cluster of 23 poppies, between the roses and the Chinese lanterns. Vary the heights. Cluster six poppies between the bark and lichen in the front left corner and add the coral.

6 Insert 12 bunches of broom bloom to add delicacy. Insert several bunches horizontally into each of the front corners, splaying the bunches out to make roughly flat, fan shapes. Insert a tall, thick cluster behind the roses, angled outwards to form a delicate frame; and small vertical bunches either side of the Chinese lanterns.

Large-Scale Dried Display

FOR HIGH-SCALE DRAMA, MAKE THIS LOW-LEVEL ARRANGEMENT OF DRIED FLOWERS AND FOLIAGE
SET IN A PEWTER VASE

For sheer impact, there's nothing like a huge, floor level display in a stunning vase. The main challenge of this easy to make display is finding a large, attractive container that suits the decor of your room, as well as your budget.

AUTUMNAL SHADES

The colour scheme is based on autumnal russets, yellows, browns and crimsons, with a strong dash of cool clear blue for pleasing contrast.

The list of ingredients is small, containing only six different flowers and foliage, but some are unusual, and you may have to make substitutions.

CHOOSING THE FLOWERS

Achillea, or yarrow, is a standard ingredient in autumnal arrangements. It comes in pale and deep gold and several more vibrant dyed colours.

Flowers or seedheads of umbellifiers, such as dill, fennel or cow parsley, give the same plate-like effect as achillea.

Huge red banksias, or Australian honeysuckle, add strong, solid form and an exotic touch, but you will probably have to order them from your florist in advance. Banksias come in many sizes and colours, often with attractive, contrasting stamens. The closely related South African proteas and dryandra (another Australian genus)

have similar-looking, rounded or cone-shaped flowers, and can be used instead of banksias.

The dried leaves and seed pods of dudinea provide density. Alternatively, you could use small branches of dried stirlingia or Mimosa.

EXOTIC TI-TREE

Ti-tree comes from the Southern hemisphere, in dyed or natural colours. Its dense mass of tiny flowers and foliage creates a heather-like effect. You could use long branches of tree heather (*Erica arborea*) instead. Other alternatives include stems of golden rod, cut to different lengths to give

PREPARING THE FOUNDATIONS

1 Weigh down the base of a lightweight container with some large stones. Crumple four or five sheets of newspaper into loose balls. Push each piece down into the vase until it is three-quarters full. Do not pack the newspaper down too tightly.

2 Put the block of florist's foam into the mouth of the vase and push it down until it is resting on the crumpled newspaper. Cut the florist's foam straight across the top so the block protrudes 2.5cm (1 in) above the vase rim. Add more newspaper if the foam is too low.

3 It is important that the foam is fixed firmly. If the mouth of the container is wider than the block of foam, cut off a small wedge of the remaining florist's foam and push this piece down into the mouth of the container so that the main block is held firmly.

MAKING A LARGE SCALE DISPLAY

1 Wedge the florist's foam tightly into the top of the urn (see box). Starting with the tallest material, the beech leaves, arrange them towards the back of the arrangement. This large-scale display will stand in a corner so create a fanning out shape, with the tallest material at the back and the shortest at the front.

4 Cut the banksia stems down so they are about 15cm (6 in) long. Before you arrange the buds, prise the leaves away from the flowers so they enhance the flower. Arrange the banksias close to the centre of the display and at the front. Place them so they fan outwards. The banksias will be focal point.

INGREDIENTS
1   *dudinea*
2   *½ bunch of wheat*
3   *4 stems of banksia*
4   *5 stems of yellow achillea*
5   *dyed beech leaves*
6   *ti-tree*
7   *pewter vase*
8   *florist's foam*
9   *scissors*

2 Cut the ti-tree stems so that they are slightly smaller than the beech leaves. While you are arranging the ti-tree, stand back from the arrangement to create a fanned look. Create blocks of colour by arranging pairs of stems together. Keep four stems to one side as fillers.

3 Use the dudinea stem to create a large block of colour to one side of your display. Remember that the display will be floor standing, so try to view it from above as you go along. The dudinea should be lower than the ti-tree and the final display should have a tiered effect.

a graduated effect; dried fringe myrtle (*Calytrix*) or alyssum.

CHOOSING THE FOLIAGE
Big branches of crimson-dyed beech leaves provide mass, a sense of movement and a pleasing natural form. Beech foliage also is available dyed a copper-russet colour, but dyed beech will need ordering in advance.

If in doubt, buy more preserved beech than you think you'll need, rather than skimp and be disappointed with the final result.

Home-glycerined beech, hornbeam, sweet chestnut and birch are equally good alternatives.

CHOOSING THE CONTAINER
The vase shown in this display is antique pewter and based on the shape of an amphora, an ancient Roman or Greek double-handled vase.

For a less formal look, consider terra-cotta chimney pots, breadbins, or even terracotta strawberry pots normally used for garden plants.

Whatever you choose, it must be heavy and secure enough not to be knocked over or tipped by the weight of the flowers and foliage. If your vase is too light, weight the base down. The vase should be narrow in proportion to its height to restrict the amount of material needed to achieve the fan-shaped effect.

CHOOSING THE SETTING
A floor-level display has the advantage of having nowhere to fall, but make sure it is in a sensible spot. Setting it against a wall protects it on one side; setting it in a corner gives double protection, and creates a stage setting.

Try to build up the display where you want it to stand, so you don't have to carry it through narrow doorways to its final location. Another advantage is that you can fill the space available exactly.

Make sure there is enough room to walk around the display, so it does not appear cramped.

If you have any frisky pets, make sure they won't be able to rush up to it and knock it over.

5 The yellow achillea brings a shock of bright colour and lifts the russet tones of the display. Arrange it so that it is medium height in the display, but close to the front. Keep a few stems of achillea spare for filling in any gaps in the arrangement later.

6 Arrange the wheat in bunches. Place the arrangement on the floor and make sure there is no florist's foam showing when it is viewed from above. For any gaps at the front of the display, use the extra pieces of ti-tree and yellow achillea. For those visible from above, use any remaining pieces of wheat.

$\mathscr{C}$REATIVE CONTAINERS

Just as you learned to look at flower colours, forms and relationships in a 'new light', and to experiment with creating refreshingly unusual combinations, it's now time to take a fresh look at containers. After all, a container can have as much impact on the eye as its floral contents, and thinking of both as a unified whole is one of the most important steps in learning to arrange flowers. The container can also help set the over-all mood: a flower-filled crystal punch bowl makes one type of statement; a flower-filled copper kettle or wicker basket makes another.

While traditional containers, such as china cherub or dolphin vases, are always useful; simple, neutral containers, such as clear glass or pottery cubes, cylinders, bowls or bottles, are easier to experiment with. They tend to be inexpensive, never look dated, and some very lovely ones, such as empty 'designer' perfume bottles, cosmetic jars and even empty food jars, can be had for free! And by collecting several identical containers, you can play the 'multiples' game: a pair of identical flower-filled vases either side of a mantelpiece; a tight trio of identical vases, each featuring one type of flower; a row of four down the middle of a dining room table – the variations are as endless as variations on a musical theme.

Our first project shows you how to make the most of transparent glass. Instead of worrying about how to hide the foundations or stems, you construct a self-contained flower arrangement on top of the container, which is filled with delicate-

ly tinted water. You'll also learn how to create a fantastically exotic display by up-ending a glass container, and using it as a prop!

ABOVE An original container that totally rings the changes are bright, shiny bell-peppers. Create an impressive buffet table design, like the featured display using peppers. Halve and hollow out the vegetables, insert soaked florist's foam and fill them with real spray carnations, yellow freesias, lady's mantle, solidago and lonicera foliage.

Clustering containers is another way to create a personal design statement. Whether you are lucky enough to have a collection of precious silver or porcelain, or simply use empty jars or oven-proof ramekins, you can mix and match to your heart's content. Large scale clusters have dramatic impact; miniature clusters are as enchanting as dolls-house furniture, and take up just as little room.

Baskets have always been firm favourites for dried-flower arranging, but by water-proofing them (we tell you how), you can use them as the basis for country-garden fresh flower displays, and widen possibilities far beyond the rather dull and rigid florist's baskets.

You can make containers out of objects you'd otherwise throw away: a cardboard shoe box completely covered with dried moss, lichens, seed pods and flowers becomes an *objet d'art* in its own right, and a splendid base for a symmetrical triangle display of dried flowers.

Objects that you would never before have considered for one moment as possible containers for flower arrangements may surprise you.

Our final project shows you how to transform a high fashion tapestry carpet bag into the huge 'vase' for a stunning collection of dried and silk flowers. It also shows how to derive your floral colour theme from the bag's fabric. Without buying a single item, you'll discover that your home is packed full of potential containers or flower displays, just waiting to be discovered!

Creative Comparisons
A GLASS VASE

Be creative with your favourite glass container – follow our lead and let your imagination run wild, and you'll find an infinite number of ways to add interest and beauty to an ordinary glass container. Here we start by using food dyes.

A rectangular glass vase can be used in different ways to bring fresh accents to your flower designs. You can turn it on its side without water and display fresh flowers and pretty shell accessories or use the vase upright and fill it with sand, pebbles, shells or coloured water.

A glass vase shows off the natural beauty of the blooms, provided the glass and water are spotlessly clean. Prevent the build-up of unattractive slime by adding a few drops of bleach to the water. These front-facing arrangements are ideal for displaying on narrow shelves, window-sills and mantelpieces.

USING FOOD DYES
Colouring the water with food dyes allows you to ring in the changes and turn a single container into one that suits all seasons and materials of all colours.

In the display featured, the stems are held in foam inserted into a weighted pinholder fixed to the container, turning the vase into a pedestal. This base lends itself to an elegant triangular flower design with gently sloping sides and graceful lines. Prolong the life of the tulips and roses by re-cutting the stems, topping up the water frequently.

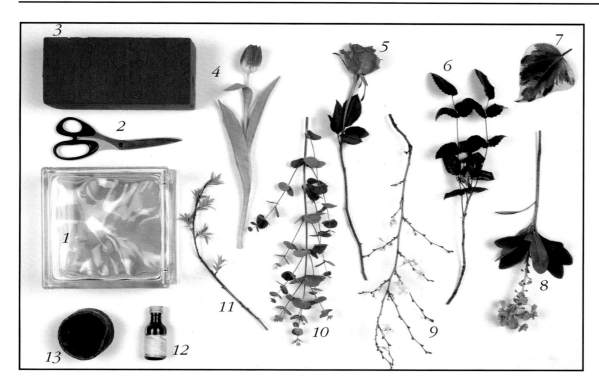

INGREDIENTS

 1 1 rectangular glass vase
 2 scissors
 3 florist's foam
 4 5 pink tulips
 5 6 pink roses
 6 1 stem of mahonia
 7 1 ivy stem
 8 4 stems of euphorbia robbiae
 9 6 flowering almond branches
10 5-6 eucalyptus stems
11 1 branch deciduous shrub
12 red food colouring
13 pinholder

FAR LEFT *Make the most of a clear glass vase by matching pink-tinted water to a graceful display of pink roses and tulips.*

1 Fill the vase two-thirds full of water and add a few drops of red food colouring. Insert a block of saturated florist's foam about 10cm (4 in) deep onto a pinholder. Place it on top of the vase on the left-hand side. Form the basic structure of the display by inserting long branches of almond into both sides of the foam. Let the branches trail down asymmetrically.

2 Hide the block of florist's foam with fresh foliage. Add a long sweep of eucalyptus stems to the right-hand side of the vase. Insert the euphorbia, mahonia, ivy and deciduous shrub stem. Cluster the large-leaved varieties to form a solid, deep-green centre. Add the lighter foliage following the line of the almond to reinforce the flowing lines.

3 Add the flowers. Trim the tulips. Curl the petals of two flowerheads by rolling the petals backward gently between your forefinger and thumb. Place the open tulips in the centre facing to one side to create a focal point. Insert three uncurled tulips to the side and centre of the display. Trim the roses and position them throughout the display to follow the line of the almond branches.

SHELLS AND ORCHIDS

The success of the featured composition with orchids and shells depends on a selection of simple accessories chosen for their contrasting shapes and interesting textures. Shells are intriguing – their pearly interiors change hue with every flicker of light and reflect the colours of their surroundings. You could use large, craggy oyster shells with their pale mother-of-pearl linings framing darker flowers or iridescent abalone. Sea-washed pebbles have their own tactile appeal.

During your summer holidays look out for pretty shells and colourful stones on the beach. They are an invaluable source of inspiration for a myriad of flower arrangements, whether they are fresh, silk, or dried. When you get any seashore treasures home, scrub them well with

water and a few drops of general household bleach.

Driftwood extends the width of the design and provides another fascinating shape and texture. If you don't have any, instead create a similar effect with a couple of gnarled twigs (apple would be ideal) or lengths of curved cane or willow. Collect your own driftwood on the beach or from under hedgerows. Tidy up broken twigs with secateurs and scrub the branch clean. Use it natural, varnish it, stain it with shoe polish, or bleach it in a bucket with a solution of domestic bleach until it turns the desired colour.

With such a glimmering and gorgeous background, the flowers must be equally special. Orchids, lilies, camellias and fully open tulips would all rise to the occasion and make a memorable arrangement. Most

ABOVE Waxy cymbidium orchids and pearly, iridescent shells contrast with the textures of twisted driftwood and dappled, sea-washed stones to form an exotic beachscape.

florists sell orchid phials which hold enough water to nourish the short stems. They are also useful to conceal in an indoor garden or a bowl of fruit, revealing a few fresh stems.

Orchids will last up to three weeks if they are looked after properly. When you buy them from the florist, ensure they are well wrapped up to protect them from cold draughts on the way home. Keep them at a steady temperature away from full sunlight. Change the water in the phials frequently and add cut-flower food to the water.

INGREDIENTS
1 1 rectangular glass vase
2 2 pieces of twisted wood
3 3 orchids in phials
4 a handful of pebbles
5 3 pearly shells
6 scissors

1 Lie the vase on its side with its mouth facing forward. Place one shell inside the mouth of the vase, tilted forward so its centre can be seen from the front. Place a second shell face down on the centre top of the vase. Balance a third shell on top, with its pearly side facing up. If necessary, secure with a piece of blue tacky clay.

2 Keep the orchids in their phials. Position one phial resting inside the shell in the mouth of the vase. Place it at a slight angle so that the orchid flowerhead faces outward, to the left. Rest the other two phials on top of the vase. Position them next to one another on the left-hand corner of the vase, forming an upward diagonal. Keep the phials stable with blue tacky clay.

3 Take the pieces of wood, both about 30cm (12 in) long, and balance ends on the vase behind the shells. Place them so their lengths extend evenly on either side of the vase. Sprinkle a handful of pebbles over the top of the vase to conceal the orchid phials.

Creative Comparisons

A NOVELTY GLASS

The three-in-one container, or trefoil, featured here shows again how versatile glass receptacles can be for both fresh and dried flower arranging. When the vases are filled almost to the brim with water, the designs have a cool, clear look, and the flower and foliage stems are an important part of the arrangement. By contrast, when the vases are filled with pot pourri, they take on an entirely different appearance, and the fragrant petals conceal the spindly and less attractive stems of the dried flowers.

The first of our three arrangements uses the minimum of plant materials, and makes a virtue of the sparse look. This is achieved by the careful choice of flower and foliage texture: the glossy purple petals of the eustoma (lisianthus) blooms contrast with the matt, down-like appearance of the senecio leaves. Other effective combinations would be long stems of freesias, tapering off to tight buds at the tip, teamed with furry green-grey ballota foliage and, in springtime, tulips or parrot tulips would look dramatic arranged in this way with stems of spiky-leaved silver *Helichrysum angustifolium* (curry plant).

A BLOOMING BUNCH
The versatility of the container is emphasised by our second floral design, a colourful bunch of flowers including bridal gladioli, *Salvia claryssa*, freesia and fuchsia. The stems are seen as a tight cluster supporting the full and generous looking array of flowerheads.

Part of this composition's charm is the choice of different flower shapes – the sharply tapering gladioli spires, the massed florets of the dramatically veined salvia, the smooth trumpet shapes of the freesia and the hanging bells of the fuchsia. When substituting other materials to display in similar designs, try to select contrasting blooms. You could choose white achillea, deep pink nerines, tiny yellow pompon dahlias and blue-mauve aquilegia.

DRIED BEAUTY AND FRAGRANCE
Our third design shows a completely different way to emphasise the beauty of the novelty container. The three glass vases are filled almost to the rim with a spicy rose petal and lavender pot pourri. The dried petals form colourful columns which blend with the pink, red and lime green of the dried stems.

Other effective dried-flower combinations would be orange carthamus with bronze dahlias and blue-dyed gypsophila, or silver-blue echinops with blue larkspur or delphinium and, in the fluffy filler role, enchanting white edelweiss or bunched pearl everlasting.

As the container takes on the colour of the pot pourri, always select your dried flowers and pot pourri mixture to match.

PERFECT STEMS

When arranging flowers in a glass container, it is important to pay scrupulous attention to plant hygiene. Strip off all the leaves that are below the water level as they will discolour and foul the water. Also they would detract from the vertical line of the stems. If you use stems with large thorns, such as roses, strip these off, using a small, sharp knife. If you fill the vases with gravel or other chippings before you insert fresh-flower stems, check the stems do not show through. If a stem is visible, use a fine skewer to ease it away from the side of the container and allow the gravel to settle against the glass.

The perfect complement to the muted hues of a golden pot pourri mixture would be a predominantly yellow arrangement. A russet-brown mixture including star anise, minute larch cones, juniper berries, shavings of cinnamon quills and verbascum flowers, would provide a harmonizing and highly textured base for an arrangement of dried seedheads such as lotus flowers, teasels and grasses.

ALTERNATIVE DEVICES
For both fresh and dried arrangements you could fill three vases with small gravel chippings, marble chippings or tiny pebbles, topping them up with water for fresh displays. To add more colour to a design, try filling the vases with water tinted with a few drops of food colouring, choosing a single colour to harmonize with the arrangement, or, for a special party look, three different colours.

If you do not have a three-in-one container, you can achieve a similar effect by grouping together three glass specimen vases or ordinary straight-sided drinking glasses and standing them on a round wooden board or a slab of grey marble.

THE RIGHT SETTING
Trefoil containers have been popular since the 18th century, when they were frequently displayed with moss roses and cabbage roses. Nowadays they are equally well suited to traditional or modern settings so there will be a place for them in any house.

When the glass vases are filled with clear or coloured water, capitalize on the dramatic effect by placing them on a desk or table in front (but not too close to) a window, or beside a lamp. For an arresting dining-table display, surround the group with short, stubby candles or glowing nightlights.

LEFT Deep purple eustoma flowers and silver-grey senecio blend strikingly in a simple composition that is perfect for a dressing table or dining table.

1 Fill each of the glass containers with water up to 5cm (2 in) from the top of the vase. Put one piece of senecio into each vase, making sure that all the leaves are stripped from the stem below the water-line to avoid rotting and water discoloration. The container is designed to be viewed all round so arrange the foliage so that it fans out.

2 Take your chosen feature flower, in this case eustoma, and strip off the lower leaves as before. Although there may be a few blooms on a single stem, you shouldn't overcrowd the container so only use one bloom in each tube. Cut the stems so that the flowers will be twice the height of the container and arrange with the senecio foliage in the tubes.

3 The blooms should be facing outwards. Keep the foliage near the outside of the display so that it enhances the flowers. Check that the display is balanced on all sides. Alternative flowers can be used, such as eucharis lilies, roses or fuchsias. For alternative foliage, choose delicate ferns, hosta, periwinkle or even sprigs of ivy.

LEFT A mass of colourful blooms and contrasting shapes – Salvia claryssa, bridal gladiolus, fuchsia and freesia make an interesting combination in an all-round design which has the charm of garden flowers.

1 Cut the stems of the *Salvia claryssa* at an angle so they are approximately one and a half times the height of the vase. Strip off any leaves that fall below the water level. Arrange two or three in each tube. Cut the fuchsia stems at an angle and place one in each tube, with the flowerheads facing outwards over the rim of the container.

2 Cut six stems of gladioli in the same way as the fuchsias. Arrange two flowers in each tube. Keep these flowers towards the centre of each tube, so that the *Salvia claryssa* encircles the gladioli. The delicate white of the flower offsets beautifully the other material you are using and offers a good contrast in shape to the other blooms.

3 Snip the stems of a bunch of yellow freesias and arrange one or two stems in each tube. As you are arranging the flowers, keep turning the container to ensure that the display can be viewed from all sides and there are no unsightly gaps. Freesias are suitable for this display due to their delicate shape and colour. White achillea, nerines or pompon dahlias are all suitable alternatives.

LEFT The three glass vases are filled with spicy pot pourri, a pretty and aromatic way to conceal the stems of dried roses, lady's mantle and paeonies.

1 Pour the pot pourri into a bowl. Taking each tube separately, fill them almost to the top with it. Make sure that each tube is filled equally, otherwise the overall design will look untidy. The pot pourri is ideal for filling this sort of container as it will hide all of the stiff, dried stems of the flowers. Choose a pot pourri that blends with the colour of the room and the flowers.

2 Cut three to six stems of lady's mantle (*Alchemilla mollis*) so they are one and a half times the height of the trefoil. Strip the lower leaves for easy insertion into the pot pourri. Arrange one or two stems into each of the tubes making sure they are completely hidden by the pot pourri. Arrange the flowers so that they look lush in the container.

3 Cut the stems of four roses and four paeonies to roughly the same length, making the roses slightly longer so their tall, elegant shapes can add interest to the display. Place at least one paeony in each of the tubes, making sure that they are all facing outwards so that the display looks balanced on all sides. Finally, arrange the rose stems, making sure the stems are hidden from view.

Multi-Vase Groupings

Displaying flowers in a group of vases gives you the chance to show off your favourite china or glassware. Whether your passion is for teapots or chamber pots, elegant Chinese porcelain or rustic wicker, now is the time to retreive those treasured objects and dust off the cobwebs. Line them up on a shelf or group them together and fill them with flowers to form an attractive focus of attention in your room.

FLOWERS IN POTS
A simple but effective idea is to use old chamber pots of different shapes and patterns as plant holders; they look good arranged on a broad windowsill, keeping your collection permanently in the limelight. To continue the theme, arrange some colourful, fresh flowers in a chamber pot, away from the window in another part of the room, perhaps on a table but within the same line of sight. A simple way to arrange flowers in a chamber pot is to crumple up some chicken wire and fix in the neck of the container to firmly secure the stems.

Another interesting object that makes a stunning vase is the teapot – many being valuable collectors' pieces coming in a variety of sizes and shapes. A small teapot bursting with a cheerful bunch of flame-coloured zinnias would look fun beside a large teapot bristling with coral-coloured sedum, especially if the pots are Art Deco style in cream, orange, black and yellow Don't neglect the spouts for individual blooms!

Tall Art Deco style vases look equally stunning with bold simple designs incorporating angular strelitzia flowers. Be sparing with the flowers or the clean design lines of such vases will be swamped under a mass of blooms, and stick to just one or two colours.

COMPOSING A PICTURE
Half the battle in flower arranging is choosing the correct display position for your design. There is no point in creating a beautiful arrangement if it's tucked away out of sight in a corner. Sit on your sofa or at your dining table and make a note of where your eyes fall. That is where the flowers should be placed to make them a prominent feature of the room.

If the focal point of the room happens to be a sideboard or shelves, try mixing your arrangement with a china collection, ornaments, pictures, candles or fruit to make them part of an interesting picture. Using a mirror or painting as a background will add to the effect.

The colours of your favourite painting could be echoed in the flower display. For a golden tableau, try a tall vase of glowing yellow rudbeckia and a few stems of *Euphorbia marginata* with its elegant pale yellow and soft green marked leaves in the background. In the front a contrasting spherical vase of a deeper colour could hold a small bunch of deep-orange pot marigolds and calendulas which could continue the daisy-petalled theme. A bowl of oranges and tangerines would complete the scene.

Consider the scent. Will people be seated near enough to appreciate it? If so, try sweet-smelling waxy stephanotis in the background and a bowl of full-blown white roses at the front. White pebbles from the beach could add the finishing touch at the base of the vase, or arrange them in a nest of bleached grasses.

It is often easier to work to a theme. For a low coffee table an idea would be the seashore. Gather a collection of attractive shells: use the larger ones as vases, or buy shell-shaped vases. Add pieces of driftwood, cork or pebbles for a selection of textures. Choose the flowers carefully, delicate blooms are best as a contrast. Use rose-buds, gypsophila or dried pink helichrysum to reflect the soft-pink pearly insides of the shells, or echo the colours of the sea: blues, greens and silver-greys. Choose from borage, lavender, sea holly, brilliant gentian or the blue-mauve *Geranium grandiflorum* with its long-stalked green leaves.

A RUSTIC NOTE
If you have wicker or old-pine furniture, a collection of dried flowers or fruits can give a more homely feel and warm up the coldest of rooms. If you have plenty of space at ground level, heap a big wicker tray with assorted gourds in vibrant gold, orange, yellow and green. If they are left in sunlight, their colours will fade slowly to muted shades, giving pleasure all winter.

Behind such a display, you could position baskets of different sizes and shapes in traditional styles full of scented lavender, Chinese lanterns and sheaves of wheat and barley. Think along the lines of a harvest festival and let your imagination run riot. For example, wind dried flowers and decorative ribbons around the hooped handles of shopping baskets. Try and find some corn dollies for a finishing touch.

ALL IN A ROW
Don't worry if you are short of space in the home. Where there is only room for a single line of vases, the limitation can be used to striking effect. A shelf is an excellent place to put a row of glass bottles or vases, especially if it is near a window so the light can reflect and refract through the glass. Mix shapes and heights to avoid a uniform look but keep to the same vessel type, whether they are the old blue chemist bottles or exotic Venetian vases. Choose feature flowers that look good in silhouette, such as ranunculus, paeonies and roses, and display one or two perfect blooms in each receptacle.

In the kitchen there are many unlikely containers that make good vases. Take tins, for instance: you can use any sort of tin, the old, ornate ones are most effective but you

can buy reproduction versions from most hardware and department stores. If using metal containers, remember not to fill them with water or they'll go rusty and leak. Instead place a jam jar inside, making sure it doesn't show above the tin. For the best effects, use garden flowers, such as poppy seedheads, day lilies and geraniums. Include herbs as the foliage.

For a table arrangement or, if you're feeling exotic, for the surround of your bath, float water lilies in wide, shallow Chinese bowls. They look refreshing and cool, even on the most humid of days. For a larger display, such as a table centrepiece, surround a large bowl with a cluster of smaller ones. To keep water lilies open once cut, drip melted wax between petals.

THE VICTORIAN LOOK
If your home is in the Victorian gothic

style, built with red bricks and embellished with turrets, dormer windows and gables, or even a converted Victorian townhouse, you can recreate an original Victorian feel by your choice of flowers and style of arrangements.

To complement velvet curtains and lace table-cloths you will need a variety of arrangements for every free space in your house. The Victorians loved clutter: wall-to-wall mirrors and pictures, tables and sideboards crowded with family photos and knick-knacks. This love of clutter also extended to their flower-arranging ideas and they would often have elaborate multi-vase groupings displayed to dramatic effect in their drawing rooms and salons.

Use genuine Victorian glass, if you can find it, and ceramic and metal containers wherever possible. A favourite Victorian vase was the epergne. Lilies, roses and

ABOVE A few bright garden flowers – anemones, pansies, calendulas, scented geranium leaves and an iris – perfectly set off this collection of glass bottles, to make an attractive multi-vase grouping.

ferns flowing over the vases make an extravagant table decoration. Fill rose bowls and small vases and dot them around the room on crocheted doilies or hand-embroidered mats on every available surface.

In the Victorian era it was essential to make your guests feel welcome by the strategic placement of flower arrangements on the dining table. On grand occasions several epergnes would be employed, with strands of fern and ivy trailing across the cloth between place settings. More discreet and practical are

tiny vases of drinking glasses holding a single bloom for each guest. Search junk and antique shops for these; you should be able to pick them up quite cheaply. Also look out for miniature flutes of striped glass on legs, perfect for holding individual flowers.

A NOSTALGIC FEEL
When choosing flowers for a Victorian arrangement it is most appropriate to opt for old-fashioned blooms such as roses, pansies, geraniums or pinks. Use plenty of delicate ferns and select foliage that is dappled or streaked and blooms with unusual shapes, such as fuchsia, antirrhinum, calceolaria and lily. For a complete Victorian feel to your home invest in plenty of pot plants like aspidistra or parlour palm and stand on cast-iron stands or dark wood pedestal tables.

DOWN TO EARTH
You can use a group of earthenware flower pots as country-style containers for growing plants and fresh or dried flowers. Remember that this type of pot is porous. When they are planted with growing plants, they will need a waterproof drip-tray such as a glazed earthenware saucer, and when they are to hold fresh flowers they will need an inner liner, such as an old beaker or a jam jar.

A collection of growing herbs in flower pots of varying sizes makes an interesting and aromatic group for a country kitchen or dining table, looks good on a pine dresser, and thrives on a sunny windowsill. Take advantage of the wide variety of leaf colours and textures and have small pots planted with, for example, golden thyme and trailing garden thyme and larger ones with bright green curly-leaved parsley,

ABOVE In this individual floral collection, the pyramid of nigella is delicate, while the haze of gypsophila surrounding the larger pot diffuses the bulk of the paeony and hydrangeas.

purple sage, sweet basil, mauve-flowering chives, and scented geranium. Clusters of cut herbs look good in flower pots, too. You could fill the lined pots to overflowing with variegated mint and lemon balm leaves and highlight them with bright blue cornflowers, marguerites and santolina flowers.

To compose an informal dried flower group, fit the neck of the pots with crumpled wire mesh and arrange them with wayside materials – wild oats, dried grasses and poppy seedheads – and a handful of pink and cream rosebuds.

Miniature Arrangements

FLOWERS THAT ARE SMALL AND DAINTY ARE PERFECT FOR THE MOST EXQUISITE MINIATURE
ARRANGEMENTS THAT PROVIDE A LARGE-SCALE IMPACT

Gypsophila is perfect for miniature displays, and a well-furnished branch supplies enough material for several arrangements. You could also use sprigs of sea lavender, which is cheaper, especially in winter.

Mimosa, with its tiny bauble-like flowers, is small and dainty enough to fit into the smallest scheme.

INTERESTING FOLIAGE

The variegated foliage of snow on the mountain is available from florists, but you may have to order it in advance. Otherwise, use the yellow or white-variegated leaves of lesser periwinkle (*Vinca minor*) or the crinkly leaves of variegated pittosporum. Tradescantia house plants need regular cutting back, to keep them bushy. Use healthy cuttings in miniature displays.

The silver box step-by-step arrangement (also overleaf) includes grape hyacinths; De Caen anemones; pink phlox; and the pink and green leaves of the polka-dot plant (*Hypoestes sanguinolenta*).

Grape hyacinths come in white, cream and various blue shades. Many spring-flowering bulbs are ideal for miniature displays, such as blue-flowered glory of the snow (*Chionodoxa*); squill (*Scilla*); and striped squill (*Puschkinia scilloides*).

Open-faced De Caen anemones come in single and double forms, in colours ranging from white and pink to scarlet, blue and deep purple.

ATTRACTIVE FILLER

Phlox provide showy clusters of white, pink, purple or lavender-blue flowers,

ABOVE Miniature silver baskets filled with delicate sprigs of gypsophila and pale-pink polyanthus are ideal for individual place settings at a spring wedding or christening meal. Line porous woven baskets with polythene, then insert saturated florist's foam block, cut to measure.

LEFT A tropical shell is filled with two spider chrysanthemums with a few buds. One stem of spray chrysanthemums should provide material for several shells. Fill the shell with water, or pack it with wet florist's foam, then insert the shortened stems.

often suffused with a contrasting colour. They are common florist flowers. Alternatives include blue-flowered Jacob's ladder (*Polemonium caeruleum*) and antirrhinums.

Many house plants with variegated or colourful foliage are small enough for miniature displays: ornamental-leaf begonias, aluminium plants (*Pilea cadierei*), tradescantias, crotons, and the velvet plant (*Gynura aurantica*).

CHOOSING THE CONTAINERS
Choose a small container, no more than 8cm (3 in) high or wide. You can build up a collection of miniature containers from empty perfume bottles, cosmetic jars and old-fashioned medicine bottles in coloured glass. Use tiny, faceted-glass food and jam jars, miniature spirit bottles and decorative tea tins. Look out for old salt shakers, stemmed glasses and egg cups at sales and bazaars.

Collect antique china or silver bowls, cigarette cases, and pill and snuff boxes, although some are too valuable to risk tarnishing or scratching. Silver-plated items and old-fashioned stoneware, such as inkwells, are cheaper and safer to use.

CHOOSING THE SETTING
Miniature displays are easily over-looked and knocked over, so take extra care in finding a suitable setting. Wall-hung, open-fronted display cabinets are excellent, providing the flowers and foliage don't project too far beyond the front face. You can sometimes buy old-fashioned wooden typesetters' boxes, to hang on the wall; or use narrow glass shelves, such as those in a modern medicine cabinet.

Although the displays need to be safe, they need to be close enough for you to appreciate the beauty of flowers. For a dinner party, set each place with a miniature arrangement.

Sometimes less is more, and the saying is true when you design a miniature arrangement. With large displays, you usually work to a preconceived, completed image. With miniature displays, you have less material to work with and more freedom to improvise, especially if you are producing several miniatures. Overleaf are two miniature displays with easy-to-follow step-by-step instructions.

CHOOSING THE FLOWERS
The milk jug arrangement (overleaf) calls for cream polyanthus, gypsophila, yellow mimosa and green and white foliage of snow on the mountain (*Euphorbia marginata*). Polyanthus (*Primula x polyantha*) come in many colours. If your florist doesn't sell cut polyanthus, buy some potted plants and cut the flowers. The more flowers you pick, the more buds are produced on the plant, provided you keep them well-watered and in a cool spot.

ABOVE Most florists sell bunches of spring violets with a ruffle of heart-shaped leaves. One bunch, with stems cut short, will fill an egg cup. This would be suitable for a breakfast tray arrangement. Violets absorb water through their petals and leaves so spray-mist them regularly to keep them fresh and long-lasting.

RIGHT Scarlet and black anemones and pink polyanthus echo the bright pattern on a laquered russian box. The broad polyanthus leaves and lacy anemone leaves make a ruffle round the base of the display.

FOUR STEPS TO A TINY DISPLAY IN A SILVER BOX

INGREDIENTS

1. *silver box*
2. *5 De Caen anemones*
3. *4 stems of pink phlox*
4. *4 sprigs of polka-dot plant*
5. *7 grape hyacinths*
6. *1 small plastic container*

1 To prevent the silver box from tarnishing, line it with a small plastic container, such as a bottle lid or plastic photographic film container. Fill the plastic container with water.

2 Trim the phlox to 10cm (4 in) and cut their stems so they can take up water. Arrange them evenly in a semicircle around the front of the container just above the rim.

3 Position the polka-dot plant leaves around the flowers to make a frame for the display. Position two leaves so that they arch over the front of the rim.

4 Arrange the 5cm (2 in) anemones so they hide the inner container. Finally, add height at the back with grape hyacinths 5-15cm (2-6 in).

FOUR STEPS TO A MILK-WHITE MINIATURE DISPLAY

INGREDIENTS

1 *4 sprigs of mimosa flowers*
2 *3 sprigs of mimosa foliage*
3 *3 sprays of white gypsophila*
4 *2 sprigs of euphorbia*
5 *5 cream polyanthus flowers*
6 *small white milk jug*

1 Fill the milk jug with water. Trim the stems of variegated euphorbia to 8-10cm (3-4 in). Place them in the jug, letting them fall to the rim to form a green background.

2 Trim the stems of mimosa flowers to 10cm (4 in). Place them in the vase so they arch to the left, right, and centre of the jug. Add more foliage towards the outside.

3 Add the 13cm (5 in) sprays of white gypsophila right around the other flowers to fill any gaps in the display and give a hazy outline to the overall shape.

4 Re-cut the polyanthus stems. Insert them in the centre of the display where their golden centres will be highlighted by the nearby mimosa flowers.

Bountiful Baskets

One of the most popular flower containers, particularly for dried flowers, is an ordinary basket.

There is something refreshing about an informal, flower-filled basket, whatever its size, shape or colour scheme. This may be because it symbolises the more relaxed pace of country life, in contrast to the hectic day-to-day lives that most of us lead. The key to success with this type of display is generosity – skimp on the flowers and the end result will be disappointing.

CHOOSING A BASKET

Most people have a basket or two tucked away in a cupboard, but they are so inexpensive that you might want to treat yourself to one especially for a dried-flower display. If you use your baskets regularly for shopping or storage, that is another good reason to invest in a new one! When buying, always keep your over-all budget in mind (pricing the flowers first is a good idea), as well as where the basket will be displayed. For a bountiful feeling on a budget, a smaller basket well-filled with flowers is always more effective than a huge basket, half empty. As a general guide, a 20-25cm (8-10 in) diameter basket creates a good impression without demanding an enormous outlay for flowers. It is also a manageable size for anyone totally new to flower arranging – you can easily finish your project in under two hours.

Most baskets are stable, but the odd 'hand-crafted' one may wobble when set down. Unless the arrangement is to be placed on top of a piece of priceless furniture, a bit of blue tacky clay tucked underneath the basket is a good solution! Round baskets are always popular for country-style arrangements, but an oval, square or rectangular one would do just as well. Some baskets, though, are more suitable for country-style displays than others; and a few are just plain difficult to work with, so when choosing yours, keep the points overleaf in mind.

COUNTRY-BASKET FLOWERS

Imagining a country-cottage garden in high summer is as good a reference point as any for choosing your flowers. Simple, daisy-like blooms automatically say 'country'. Here, white-and-yellow rhodanthe is combined with pink helichrysum, another member of the daisy, or *Compositae*, family. Both are 'everlastings' or 'immortelles', so-called because they have thin, papery petals and are easily dried. Mixing cultivated grains with flowers is also certain to create a country feel. In this display, wheat and larkspur, an old-fashioned, cottage-garden favourite, provide a linear contrast to the round, daisy-like flowers. *Statice dumosa* is a form of sea lavender – not technically a country plant in origin, but happy in sunny country gardens with well-drained soil.

BUYING YOUR FLOWERS

The flowers chosen for this display are relatively inexpensive and widely available, though you may have to shop around to find single-colour bunches of helichrysum. You can reproduce this combination of flowers and colours exactly, or choose different ones, according to taste, availability or budget. If you do use different flowers, make sure you still include the three main shapes: round, linear and lacy. Here, they are used in roughly equal proportions; again, you may want to follow this 'recipe', or create your own variation. But be warned: an arrangement composed largely or entirely of spiky material is more likely to look unruly than attractive.

COUNTRY COMBINATIONS

There are countless possible combinations

LINING A BASKET

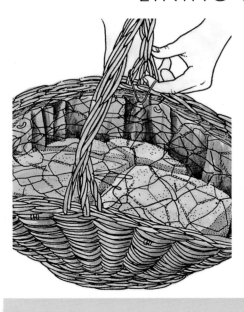

1 Line the inside of the basket with half a plastic binliner. Secure the plastic to the basket with pieces of wire bent into a hair pin shape. At regular intervals push each wire from the outside through the basket weave and the plastic lining and twist the ends together inside the basket.

2 Place two large, rectangular blocks of soaked florist's foam into the basket to cover the basket base completely. The foam is held in position by its own weight so prongs are not required.

3 Fold 1m (3 ft) of chicken wire into a cylindrical shape to fill the mouth of the basket and place in position. Secure it to the basket handle with stub wire, as before.

4 Pull up the top of the chicken wire to form a dome and set the shape of the display. Open out the holes in the chicken wire so that you can insert the flowers and foliage more easily.

of country flowers, but, as a general guide, barley could be used instead of wheat, gypsophila could be substituted for statice; and xeranthemums and ammobiums are used instead of rhodanthe and helichrysum. It is a bit more difficult to replace the clear-blue spikes of larkspur, but you might try dried aconite, or monkshood. Alternatively, the green or crimson spikes of love-lies-bleeding, or amaranthus, would add an unusual touch.

If you live in the country, try including a handful of dried wild grasses. Even a few dried garden weeds, such as polygonum or ground elder seedheads can add a pleasantly rural touch.

Avoid very obvious exotics – they may be attractive, but are more suitable for sophisticated displays.

CHOOSING THE FLOWER SHADES

Almost any colour combination can have 'country' overtones: pinks, blues, creams and whites, as here; creams and whites alone; or rich, golden autumnal tones, for example. Harsh, dyed colours can be tricky, though, and may give a 'manufactured' appearance to your display.

Repeating the colour scheme of the room in which the arrangement will be displayed is one possibility; using a contrasting colour scheme another. Or you can gear your colours to a season: the pastels and deep primary colours of spring and summer; or the russets, golds and browns of autumn. Displaying a country basket of summery dried flowers in autumn or winter can be a powerful antidote to the cold-weather blues.

CHOOSING A SETTING

A country basket adds a welcoming touch to an entrance hall, covered porch or guest bedroom, but the display is informal enough to fit comfortably almost anywhere. Try a round country basket as a centrepiece for a round or oval dining-room table; a square or rectangular one for a square or oblong one. A narrow country basket would look lovely in front of a mantelpiece mirror; one featuring lavender would pleasantly scent a bathroom. A huge country basket could be displayed at floor level, out of the way of main passages. As with any dried-flower display, keep country baskets away from bright sunlight to prevent the colours fading, and away from fireplaces that are in use as they are highly flammable.

WATCHPOINTS FOR BASKETS

● Loosely woven baskets may not conceal the foam block, so go for the tighter weaves.
● Painted or colour-sprayed baskets can be successful, particularly those in pastel shades, but for a traditional country effect, choose a basket in a natural colour, or perhaps bleached almost white. Plastic baskets are rarely attractive, whatever the style.
● Avoid narrow-based, wide-rimmed baskets, which tend to create an awkward, pinched effect. Visually, the weight is transferred downwards to an unacceptably small base, and such baskets look unstable, whether or not they actually are.
● Very shallow baskets can be effectively used for certain types of flower displays, such as tiny bouquets or posies, but for a generous looking arrangement, choose a basket deep enough to be practical. If it has a well-used, old-fashioned appearance, so much the better!
● The handle should look strong yet graceful and, for this type of display, extend well above the basket. Avoid baskets with handles that splay out from the base; this style has a rather awkward appearance that detracts from the overall shape of the arrangement.
● For a display in a dark corner, choose a pale-coloured basket, otherwise your work will disappear into the shadows.

A SIMPLE BASKET ARRAY

INGREDIENTS
 1 rhodanthe
 2 wheat
 3 larkspur
 4 helichrysum
 5 statice dumosa
 6 basket
 7 block of dry florist's foam
 8 fine gauge stub wire
 9 reel wire
10 knife
11 florist's scissors

1 Place your flowers, container and tools on a clean, dry, level surface such as a kitchen counter workshop or table. Start by wedging the foam block firmly into the basket (see box). Leave 2.5cm (1 in) of foam block projecting over the top of the basket. This allows you to insert the flowers at any angle, thus avoiding the 'explosive' look of rows of straight stems all steeply angled upwards.

2 First group the wheat heads into twos or threes – visually more effective and quicker than inserting them one at a time. Make two fan shapes, one going from front to back of the basket, and one going from side to side. The strong wheat stems are easy to insert; push them into the foam block as far as the heads. This should give you a height one to one and a half times the height of the basket but still leave sufficient room under the handle.

3 Next, fill out the basic shape with individual spikes of deep blue larkspur, evenly spaced, to add visual depth to the arrangement. Position them randomly, but as you insert the flowers, turn the basket round to look at it from all angles, making sure you are building up an even density of colours and textures. Use the two wheat 'fans' which divide the foam block into equal quarters as a guide.

MEASURING YOUR FOAM BLOCK

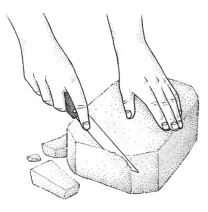

1 To measure a foam block, so it exactly fits your basket, press the basket base firmly onto the foam block so that it leaves a visible imprint.

2 Cut around the imprint left on the foam block using a sharp kitchen knife. If the sides of the basket are angled, adjust the angle you cut at accordingly.

3 There is no need to fix the foam block with a prong or adhesive – wedged tightly into your basket, it should hold firm.

4 Rhodanthes have brittle stems, so use stub wire to bind four to six flowers together, and form clusters. Keeping the tension tight, wrap the wire about six times round the stems, covering half their length. Trim the remaining stem back to just above the wire, which then becomes the new 'stem'. Make 10-12 clusters, then push them evenly into the foam.

5 Follow the same process with the pink helichrysum, but this time use only three flowers to make up each cluster, rather than four to six. Insert these at evenly spaced intervals, again, checking as you go for any large empty spaces, and re-adjusting positions if necessary. Try filling gaps with single helichrysums – the flowerheads are large enough not to stand out in a peculiar fashion when inserted singly.

6 Don't worry about the smaller patches of foam block that are still visible. They can be filled with the statice, again bunched together in tight clumps of four to six stems. Statice is an excellent 'filler', because its lacy quality prevents the arrangement becoming too dense and heavy looking. Take a final, critical look, turning the basket slowly round – you should be pleased with your handiwork!

Flower-filled Box

FOR AN ELEGANT CHANGE FROM THE ORDINARY, MAKE THIS SYMMETRICAL FLOWER
ARRANGEMENT IN ITS OWN MOSS-COVERED CONTAINER

Flower arrangements often have a few trailing stems breaking the line of the rim, but this impressive display goes to extremes, with quite dramatic results. Dried mosses, lichens, flowers and seed pods cover the container completely, transforming a modest cardboard box into a richly textured *objet d'art*. Although this project is more time consuming than many other arrangements, you don't have to shop for an expensive or elusive vase, and you can achieve a designer look without spending a fortune.

The box holds a dry florist's foam block, supporting a symmetrical, all-round, triangular arrangement of flowers, grains and ribbons. You can decorate the box and make the floral display in one sitting, or make the box and put it away until you have time to arrange the flowers.

A glue gun is shown in the step-by-step instructions, and using one is the quickest way to fix the moss and lichens to the box. If you want to buy a glue gun, choose one that guides the glue through the nozzle using a trigger device, rather than one in which the glue has to be pushed through by hand. The trigger action guns are slightly more expensive but are less messy and easier to operate. If you haven't got a glue gun, use fabric glue instead.

CHOOSING THE TINTS
The featured display is pastel and multi-coloured, with the cool silvers of moss and lichen enhanced by pink, green, white, gold, lavender and purple. You could make the display in white plus one other colour – perhaps tints of yellow, pink, lavender or blue – or all white. For a rich effect, choose autumnal shades of russets, oranges, browns and crimsons; and for Christmas, choose red, green, silver and gold materials, lightly spraying the decorated box with a metallic spray paint.

For further colour ideas, look at the wallpaper, curtains or upholstery in the room where you intend to display the box for inspiration. You can copy the combinations of colours, in the same proportions, or create your own.

DECORATING THE BOX
A dense, tapestry-like mixture of dried Spanish moss, reindeer moss and lichen is shown, studded with love-in-a-mist seed-heads and lavender spikes. You may have to order the mosses in advance, but if you live in the country or have access to woodlands, you can buy just the Spanish moss and collect and dry native mosses and lichen for extra cover. Alternatively, decorate the whole box with mosses and lichens you have collected yourself.

SPANISH MOSS
Spanish moss (*Tillandsia usneoides*) is not technically a moss, but a rootless, flowering plant closely related to the air plants that are so popular. Its thread-like stems are covered with minute, silvery scaly leaves and in its native tropical swamps, Spanish moss drapes over the branches of rocks and tall trees with tangled festoons, 6m (20 ft) or more long.

Tillandsias are epiphytic perennials that need hot, humid conditions to thrive.

It's tiny green flowers are rarely produced in cultivation. You may have to buy a larger quantity of Spanish moss than is needed here, but the remainder always can be put to good use as a filler or camouflage in dried-flower displays; and tiny pieces can be incorporated into dried-flower pictures.

USING REINDEER MOSS
Technically, reindeer moss is a lichen: a symbiotic relationship between fungi and algae. It grows wild in damp areas at high altitudes in cool temperate climates, and a similar-looking lichen can be collected from heaths, moors and lowland bogs. Reindeer moss also is harvested commercially on a vast scale in arctic and sub-arctic regions, where it is the main food of reindeer, and that is how it gets its name.

Reindeer moss is sold in natural silver grey, as shown, and other dyed colours. If the bases of the moss clumps are discoloured or caked with soil, snip them off using a pair of florist's scissors; stick the moss around the box and over the florist's foam to disguise it.

Dried bun moss can be substituted for one of the mosses shown, or used on its own. It is available from florists, but is more easily collected than other mosses, and can be found on shady banks, wall coping and roofs, even in built-up areas.

Alternatively, use dried sphagnum moss instead of one or all of the featured mosses. However, its beige colour may not be quite as pleasing with clear, soft pastels as the silvery or green mosses.

WILD LICHENS
The flat, silvery and attractively ruffled lichens shown probably will have to be collected from the wild, but they are optional. Look for them on the trunks and branches of larch and fruit trees, in mixed woodlands, and on walls and rocks. Bring a sharp knife with you when lichen hunting, and handle them with care, since they are very thin and fragile, and can shatter very easily. Often, silvery lichen is found growing on dead wood, but be very careful not to damage the bark of living trees when removing lichen from it.

Love-in-a-mist, or nigella, is used to stud the moss-covered box, helping to conceal

CONCEALING THE BOX

1 Spread glue over each side of the box in turn and affix Spanish moss, covering as much as you can. Apply adhesive to the bottom of the reindeer moss and stick it onto the Spanish moss in small, well-spaced clumps. Use sufficient glue to secure the clumps.

2 Attach pieces of lichen all over the box. It is easier if you apply the glue to the moss rather than to the lichen. Position the lichen in between the clumps of reindeer moss. Cover up any gaps. Alternatively, you could use bark or dried ivy.

3 Break the heads off half a bunch of love-in-a-mist stems, leaving a small section of stem as this will make gluing easier. Tease the love-in-a-mist heads into the gaps in the Spanish moss. For a more colourful effect, use dried helichrysum heads instead.

4 Cut the lavender stems to 2.5cm (1 in). Apply glue to small areas of the Spanish moss and attach the lavender heads. Weave the lavender heads into the moss so they are at an angle rather than lying flat. Glue a few of the heads horizontally around the outside edge of the box.

it and providing contrast in texture. You could use poppy seedheads instead, in various sizes, and in natural silver for a subtle effect, or in colours dyed to match the flowers. Burdock thistles are another option and, with their tenacious spines, probably would stick naturally to the mossy base without the aid of glue.

FRAGRANT LAVENDER

Lavender spikes are woven amongst the moss and lichen and decorate the rim of the box, adding fragrance as well as colour. If you have heads of lavender with broken stems, this is an ideal use for them. Small sprigs of dried mint flowers from the garden could be used instead or, for a silvery touch, sprigs of dried artemisia, with its pungent, strong, clean scent.

You can glue a few delicate dried rose-buds to the moss, or lavender, helichrysum or love-in-a-mist seedheads to provide unity between the arrangement and the covered container. Alternatively, try studding the moss with attractive pebbles, shells or small bits of bracket fungi.

FLOWERS FOR THE ARRANGEMENT

Although the box and its floral contents operate as a visual unit, the triangular arrangement should be attractive enough in its own right to be effective even in a modest container.

Most of the featured flowers are available at florists, and substitutes are suggested below. If you use completely different flowers, choose small-scale, delicate ones, which have an interesting range of shapes.

Dried, pink spray rose-buds set the height and mark the centre of the design, but you could use white, peach or pale yellow dried rose-buds, or single rose-buds, instead. Use dried carthamus buds or strawflowers in peachy pink or another pastel colour. To continue the silver theme of the box up through the flowers, use smallish heads of dried echinops. You may have to wire the stems first, otherwise the top-heavy thistles tend to droop.

Perennial sea lavender, in natural white, is used as a filler, especially around the sides. It is also cheap, and even stockists of just the basic dried flowers carry it.

Alternatively, you could use dyed sea lavender or gypsophila in white or dyed colours, or dried alyssum or cress from the wild.

Statice is an annual which is closely related to sea lavender, and is equally inexpensive and as widely available. If you cannot obtain an all-purple bunch, buy a couple of mixed bunches, and use the purple, lavender, pink and white flowers. Save the other blooms for another display, or combine them in a vase with any sea lavender, wheat and love-in-a-mist left-over from this one to create a complementary arrangement which can be positioned alongside the box to continue the theme.

FLUFFY WHITE
Baby everlasting adds lightness to the display, and helps unify the pink roses with the white of the sea lavender and silvery white lichen. A typical fluffy-headed Compositae flower, you could replace it with stems of dried anaphalis, lachnostachys or miniature, white-flowered helichrysum.

Wheat ears provide spikiness to sharpen the silhouette, but any similar-sized grain could be used, in pale green or mature gold.

CHOOSING THE RIBBON
Compressed, raffia natural-fibre ribbons in pink and red are featured. In some arrangements, they're left compressed and used in sinuous curves to add a sense of movement. In other places, they're teased out to add traditional, ribbon-like softness and to provide strong areas of colour.

You can use just one colour, or hanks of plain raffia, but try to avoid florist's polyester ribbon, which is too shiny and artificial-looking for this display.

CHOOSING THE CONTAINER
A cardboard box is used, but a shoe box or metal biscuit tin would be just as suitable.

If you wish to reproduce this symmetrical triangular design, but don't want to decorate a box, build up the display in a traditional shallow dish or basket, or buy a flat, plastic florist's foam block holder from your florist. In the latter case, cut the foam block in half, and use extra sea lavender to conceal the sides of the block.

You can scale-down the project, using attractive perfume cartons and cut-down foam blocks. These would make the perfect arrangements to sell at a school fête or church bazaar, or to add an individual note of interest placed at each setting at a winter dinner party.

CHOOSING THE SETTING
The display in the moss-covered box has all the elements of a country-style composition – native mosses, cottage-garden flowers and seedheads and ears of corn. And yet, as the photograph on page 163 shows, it looks custom-made for a modern setting; which only goes to show how versatile dried-flower arrangements can be.

ABOVE This plaited straw box contains a charming mixture of dried selaginella (fern moss), sea lavender, strawflowers and tansy. The natural-fibre ribbon adds broad bands of colour.

With the horizontal side stems, the trails of furled raffia ribbon and its generally 'busy' look, the design needs space if it is to be fully appreciated. This arrangement would look particularly well in the centre of a sideboard, on top of a low cupboard or side table, or on a long, low table at the foot of a bed. Candlelight or the soft glow of a table lamp will further flatter both the soft colours and the romantic mood of the design.

CREATING A DRIED-FLOWER DISPLAY SET IN A MOSSY BOX

1 Cut a block of foam to fit the mossy box; the foam should protrude by 1-2cm (½-1 in). Cover the florist's foam with a layer of the remaining reindeer moss. You can hold the moss in place using the stub wire. Bend the wire in half then push it into the foam.

4 Choose the longest stems of baby everlasting and arrange them in the centre of the box. If you find that the stems are too short, attach florist's wire to make them longer. Arrange the shorter stems at angles to give the arrangement a fan shape. The baby everlasting will enhance the soft pink of the dried roses.

INGREDIENTS

1 1 bunch of dried roses
2 ½ bunch of baby everlasting
3 1 bunch of statice
4 ½ bunch of love-in-a-mist
5 ½ bunch of sea lavender
6 ¼ bag of lichen
7 ½ bunch of corn
8 ½ bag of Spanish moss
9 ¼ bag of reindeer moss
10 ½ bunch of lavender
11 box
12 block of florist's foam
13 glue gun
14 scissors
15 stub wires
16 raffia ribbon

2 Cut one bunch of dried roses to a length of 12cm (5 in). Arrange stems vertically in the centre of the box. Arrange the remainder so they create a fan shape. Bear in mind that this display is designed to be viewed from all angles, so arrange the flowers evenly.

3 Cut about eight pieces of raffia ribbon to between 25cm and 50cm (10in and 20in) long. Untwist the ribbon in places to create a softer effect. Loop the raffia twice around your hand and wrap a piece of stub wire tightly around one end of the loop to make a stem. Push this into the side of the foam.

NATURAL COVER

Covering boxes and other containers with moss is a way of bringing the most mundane or utilitarian articles into high profile, and creating a range of individual flower holders that will give a new personality to your arrangements.

Once you have experienced how easy it is to cover the box shown on these pages, you can develop the technique in other ways. To create the agricultural equivalent of a moss garden, take a plain wooden fruit or vegetable box, or a cardboard shoe box – depending on the size and scale appropriate to your room – and cover the sides with a blend of moss and lichen in the way described. Add textural interest by sticking on cones, eucalyptus and, if you can obtain them, small dried fungi. Fill the box with blocks of dry florist's foam, cover it with moss and arrange a bunch of wheat stalks, of even height and close together, vertically, as if they were growing. Scatter a few small cones or dried leaves between the stalks to further the pastoral illusion and place the box close to a window. Shafts of golden sunlight will not harm these partiuclar components, and will do much to enhance the display.

To adapt the idea for a Christmas arrangement, cover a shallow box with green-dyed moss, which you can buy at florists' shops. Fill the opening with florist's foam and arrange spiky stems of yew and rosemary, glittering honesty and, for a festive touch, red-dyed poppy seedheads and sprigs of holly.

As an alternative to moss and lichen, you can use hay as a fragrant and evocative covering material. Take handfuls of hay to cover tall or large containers such as upright boxes, buckets and wastepaper baskets to create floor-standing arrangements of, say, twigs, pampas grass, reeds, bulrushes and teasels, or to cover and line a round box or tub to fill with painted or dyed eggs and little vases of primroses as an Easter-nest table decoration. And for a harvest or Thanksgiving display, tie bundles of hay with raffia to cover a cornucopia-shaped dolly or basket, and fill it with polished apples and pears and sprays of orange Chinese lanterns, to create a glowing display of autumn bounty.

5 Keep the stems of the sea lavender long and use their splayed shape to fill some of the gaps. Use mainly at the sides. Arrange the corn in small groups for impact. Use the corn for its height at the centre of the design. Position small bunches at the sides.

6 Add the statice so it is close to the centre of the arrangement. Keep the lavender stems long; place in the centre of the display so they fan outwards. Also position some at the sides. Finally, take four or five pieces of coiled raffia ribbon, wire them and push them into the florist's foam at either end of the box.

A Bagged Display

TAKE YOUR LEAD FROM A TAPESTRY BAG TO CREATE AN UNUSUAL FLOOR-LEVEL DISPLAY

OF SILK AND DRIED FLOWERS

In this arrangement the container is the vital ingredient, as it is the tapestry carpet-bag that sets the scale, tone and colour scheme for the display and provides the inspiration for the choice of silk and dried flowers, branches and assorted seed pods.

SUPPORTING THE STEMS
The project is a large, floor-level, front-facing display, incorporating both silk and dried flowers, seed pods and twigs, arranged informally in a tapestry holdall or carpet-bag. The bag is padded out with shredded tissue paper – crumpled tissue paper or newspaper could also be used – not only to support the sides but also to raise the level of the base. A florist's-foam block taped to a plastic tray rests securely on the tissue paper base. The foam block serves as the foundation of the arrangement, but the sides of the carpet-bag also help to support the stems of the ingredients.

CHOOSING THE CONTAINER
A lined tapestry carpet-bag, 40cm (16 in) high and 30cm (12 in) across, is used for the featured display. Modern carpet-bags are made of new fabric, but the traditional sort were made out of old pieces of carpet. Carpet-bags are sold at department stores and handbag and accessory shops, in a range of sizes and prices. You sometimes can find old carpet-bags, in soft, faded colours, from bazaars or second-hand shops. Holidays abroad, especially in hot climates, are often a good source of hand-crafted fabric satchels or holdalls. Alternatively, use a woven straw or wicker container, perhaps with stripes of soft pastels rather than a floral motif, to provide the colour inspiration for the flowers.

For a more modern interpretation of the same theme, use a thick, clear plastic fashion bag, lining it with dried sphagnum or reindeer moss first. Alternatively, use a shallow holdall and rest the florist's foam block and tray directly in the base. For a child's room, you could use an inexpensive canvas school-bag in bright, primary colours to match the decor of the room. Hang the bag on a wardrobe door, on the wall or from the top of a bunk-bed.

CHOOSING THE SILK FLOWERS
Go to a good stockist, preferably a silk flower specialist, to obtain good value, natural-looking silk flowers. Take the carpet-bag with you for colour reference and spend plenty of time choosing flowers in complementary shades. The flowers shown are naturalistic, but good-quality 'fantasy' flowers also could be used.

Try to choose flowers in a range of shapes and sizes. If you can only find flower stems with artificial-looking foliage then remove the leaves altogether and increase the amount of dried material accordingly.

NATURAL EFFECTS
The mid-blue silk irises are especially convincing in the featured display. They have a delicate graduation of deep to pale colour, and bright-yellow, furry 'beards' on their lower petals. Silk irises come in deep-blue, yellow and white. If you can't get silk irises, try silk scabious.

Silk alstroemeria, or Peruvian lilies, add a soft pink touch. Silk double hollyhocks are perhaps the most realistic of all. The lowest flowers are fully open, gradually becoming smaller further up the stem, with the uppermost flowers in tight bud.

CHOOSING THE BRANCHES
The twiggy, sculptural branches of man-zanita are used to build up height and density in the arrangement. Manzanita (*Arctostaphylos manzanita*) is a moderately hardy shrub, related to rhododendrons and heathers.

You may have difficulty getting hold of manzanita, either as cut branches or as a garden plant. Fortunately, there are many trees and shrubs, both wild and cultivated with equally sculptural branches. As well as curly willow and contorted hazel, ordinary hazel, oak, birch, hornbeam or alder are all suitable, if less twisted, alternatives. For colour as well as sculptural interest, use red or yellow-barked branches of dogwood or willow, or the knobbly, black twigs of an old mulberry tree.

DRIED FLOWERS AND SEED PODS
The colour scheme is predominantly pink and white, with touches of green, blue and crimson, to match the colour of the carpet-bag. Study the colour proportions in your own bag and repeat them in the flowers. As well as matching the colours of individual flowers, pick up on tiny flecks of colour, a yellow tapestry flower centre for example and echo this with one or two yellow flowers in the display.

Deep-crimson amaranthus, or love-lies-bleeding, is stocked by most large dried-flower retailers. It also comes in a natural olive green. An unusual, greeny-pink alternative would be wild polygonum (knotweed) seed pods.

Silvery white, peeled honesty seed pods are included for their delicacy, their unusual, flat, disc-like shape and ability to reflect light. Alternatively, use unpeeled honesty pods in matt shades of green or wine-red.

Pink-dyed sea lavender is more difficult to obtain than natural, white sea lavender. Either paint your own with floral spray-

CREATING A BAG DISPLAY

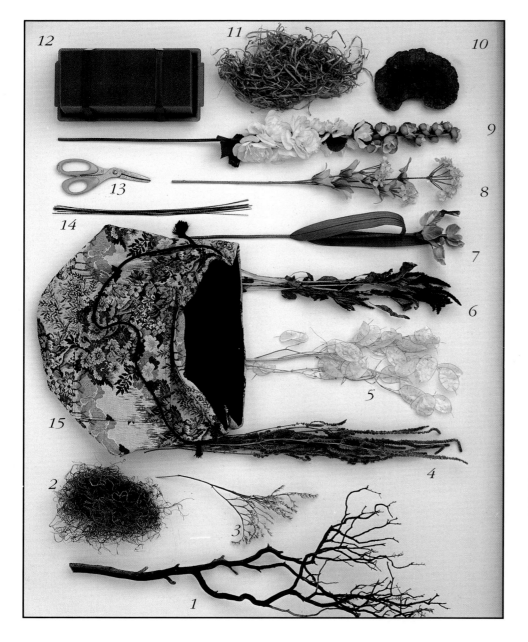

1 Pad out the bottom and sides of the carpet-bag with shredded tissue paper so that the foam block sits high up inside the bag. Tape a block of dry florist's foam to a plastic tray and place inside the bag on top of the shredded tissue. Push the foam down inside until it feels secure.

4 The dried material does not need to be either wired or cut. Separate out ten stems of pale-purple Russian statice and ten stems of dark-purple amaranthus. Insert them throughout the display at even intervals. The spiky dried florets contrast with the round silk flowerheads and the dark-purple amaranthus stems link with the bag's pattern.

INGREDIENTS

1 1 manzanita twig
2 2 handfuls of Spanish moss
3 8 stems of pink-dyed sea lavender
4 10 stems of Russian statice
5 4 stems of honesty
6 10 stems of purple amaranthus
7 5 stems of silk irises
8 4 stems of silk lady's mantle

9 2 stems of silk hollyhocks
10 5 plates of purple-dyed bracket fungi
11 shredded tissue paper
12 block of florist's foam attached to a tray
13 scissors
14 stub wires
15 carpet-bag

2 Cut a sculptured manzanita twig to a height twice the height of the bag and insert it into the middle of the foam. Turn the twig so that the most attractive side is facing forwards. Cut down four stems of pink-dyed sea lavender and insert them into the foam to fill out the entire opening of the bag and reach halfway up the length of the twig stem.

3 Continue with the silk material. Insert three silk hollyhock stems, one on either side of the central manzanita twig and one slanting forwards. Insert four silk lady's mantle stems to fill out the centre of the bag. Frame this central grouping with five stems of silk irises.

paint or replace with white or pink-dyed dried gypsophila.

Russian, or rat's-tail, statice is related closely to sea lavender although it is a different shape. Its long, pink flower spikes add height and a linear quality to the display. Use dried rose-bay willow herb or garden mint flower spikes, both in soft pinky-mauve, instead.

When all the other ingredients are in position, soft mounds of dried Spanish moss are used to bulk out the display and conceal the stub wire and plastic-coated wire stems. Dried reindeer moss, in natural silvery-grey or dyed shades, is equally suitable.

Purple-dyed bracket fungi may be the hardest ingredient for you to obtain. If necessary, order ordinary dried bracket fungi, in natural silvery-grey, and colour it purple yourself using watercolours or artist's ink.

CHOOSING THE SETTING

Any floor-level display should be large enough to make a prominent feature and sturdy enough not to be easily knocked over. This arrangement meets both criteria. A broad shelf or table against a wall would be suitable, or a stool or antique high chair positioned in a corner.

HANGING THE DISPLAY

Large, old-fashioned entrance halls are traditional locations for a collection of wicker shopping baskets and fabric hold-alls. If your home has a generous-sized entrance hall, use it to show off this arrangement. Hang it up on a brass wall hook or a coat rack, or rest it on a trunk or large hall table.

If you choose to hang the display on a wall, wardrobe door or the back of the door, make sure that the handles of the bag are fixed securely. This is most important for bigger arrangements, such as . the carpet-bag display, that hold large amounts of plant material. If you hang this display, or a smaller version, on a door that is in frequent use, fix the bag to the door using blue tacky clay. Otherwise, the arrangement will be knocked about every time the door opens, and accidental breakages will be inevitable.

5 Wire up the purple-dyed bracket fungi by pushing a single stub wire through the base of the plate and twisting it round to form a stem. Break up the stems of honesty. Insert one stem vertically and two stems towards the back. Insert the wired fungi plates around the front edge of the bag and bend the wire stems so that most lie horizontally.

6 Tease apart two handfuls of dried Spanish moss into elongated clumps and place them in position around the edge of the carpet-bag. The moss adds bulk to the display and also disguises the unsightly support wires holding the bracket fungi in position.

CHAPTER SIX

ENTERTAINING WITH FLOWERS

The presence of flowers always makes meal-times more pleasurable, whether it's an elegant, special-occasion arrangement for a luncheon, drinks or dinner party, or a simple basketful of dried flowers, gourds and seed pods that stays on the family kitchen table all winter long. This chapter concentrates on party flowers, since social events are an excuse to spend a little more time and money on flowers and foliage, and to introduce an element of drama, formality or extravagance that might look out of place in daily life.

Low, all-round displays are traditional for dining tables, since they can be appreciated from every seat, and allow table conversation to take place without having to strain to see your conversation partner. Long, narrow rectangular tables can also take triangular or oval central displays, provided they're low, and for dining tables pushed against a wall, a front-facing display, tucked against the wall, is an option.

All-round arrangements are also ideal for coffee tables, although these tend to be lower and therefore you look down more onto the flowers, a point to remember when planning your display. Food-laden buffet tables, sideboards and wedding-cake tables call for large-scale, extravagant flower displays, to draw attention to the food and act as focal points for the whole room. (Small arrangements tend to get lost visually, and tipped over in the rush to fill plates!)

Incorporating candles and fruit into floral centrepieces is emphasized in this chapter. Both of these 'accessories' are inexpensive, widely available and, combined with flowers, instantly convey a special, festive feeling. Other floral options to emphasize the importance of the occasion include repeating the main flowers in a garland looped along the table front, in the case of food tables, or, for a wedding or christening cake, placing a flower-filled bud vase on top of the cake, again repeating the flowers used in the main arrangement.

As well as using candles, whose soft

ABOVE Cool, cream flowers are bathed in warm, golden candle-light making an ideal party-table arrangement.

glow enhances flower colour and form, consider general room lighting as a potential source of drama. Simply positioning a table display under a centrally hung light shows it to best advantage, but remember that most light bulbs give off heat, so put the flowers in position at the last moment, or keep the lights turned off until needed. If you have flexible track lights, adjust one to illuminate your table flowers from across the room, for high drama.

Whatever the shape, style or size of the display, never let the florist's foam block show. Examine the display, as you build it up, from a seated position as well as a standing one, and try it out where it is to go. Use extra foliage, if you run out of flowers, snipping a single branch into short lengths, if necessary, and tucking the leafy sections close together to hide the foam. Lastly, however beautiful your display, don't let it hang over (or into!) the food, and make sure the diners have enough room to eat comfortably.

Always consider the flower arrangements you create as a significant colour accessory to the room as a whole, or to the table in particular. You may decide to compose an arrangement that echoes the colours in your furnishing fabric, tablecloth or dinner mats, or you may opt for a well-planned contrast. A bowl of bright golden marigolds, for example, would add a touch of warmth in a room decorated mainly in cool shades of grey, whereas an all-white arrangement of fragrant lily-of-the-valley could be refreshing in more colourful surroundings.

Creative Candlecups

Candles, so much a part of Christmas tradition, can be incorporated in your flower arrangements at any time of year to create an extra-special arrangement.

A candelabrum is easily converted into a holder for flowers and foliage by the simple addition of a candlecup obtainable from florist shops.

CANDLECUPS

Candlecups are shallow, bowl-like containers with a short stem or knob underneath that fits into a narrow-necked base, creating a pedestal-like effect. Traditionally inserted into candelabra, they can also fit into wine bottles or narrow-necked vases. Candlecups hold a florist's foam block, so a

much larger and more graceful flower arrangement can be constructed, than would be possible using the base alone. Candlecups are usually plastic, but can be metal, and come in black, white, green or gold. You can make your own candlecups by glueing cut-off, spray-painted yoghurt cartons to a cork, using strong glue. Candlecup knobs do vary in size, so before buying one, first measure the diameter of the candelabrum cavity. A small to medium cup is better than a large one.

If you don't own a candleabra, the candlecup can be inserted in the neck of a bottle. When the florist's foam is in place, a candle can be added before the flowers are arranged.

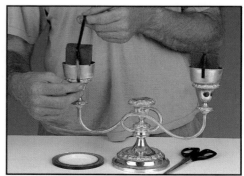

1 To secure the candlecup use a pencil-thin length of florist's mastic. Fix to follow the circular shape of the cup base and press firmly onto the candlestick opening.

2 Place florist's foam in the cup and tape securely. (To remove cup, gently twist off. Pull off the florist's foam fix and clean the candelabrum with a proprietary polish.) Attention to scale should be considered. A

spray carnation is large enough, a gerbera bloom overlarge. Spray chrysanthemums and spray carnations have several flowerheads on the main stem, so can be cut up into smaller pieces. Ivy trails prettily hides florist's foam.

Creative Comparisons
CANDLEHOLDERS

Until the advent of gas and electricity, candles were part of ordinary life, but now they are used mainly for formal or festive occasions. Their soft, flattering light creates a romantic atmosphere, especially when combined with flowers. Variations in height, and the contrast between the vertical candles and the horizontally arranged flowers are featured in the three designs.

DECORATIVE CANDLEHOLDERS
Candleholders range in design from simple to ornate and from inexpensive, mass-produced items to priceless antiques. However, cost and beauty aren't necessarily related. Inexpensive, simple candlesticks often are more effective when combined with flowers; heavily ornate ones may compete with the flowers for attention.

Transparent glass and crystal candleholders, such as those shown in two of the displays featured, are especially elegant as the flowers and candles seem to float above the table surface. Simple porcelain, brass or silver candlesticks can look equally attractive; and for more informal occasions, earthenware or wooden candleholders could be used.

A cork-shaped piece of florist's foam wedged into a candleholder is enough foundation for a small display. For a larger floral arrangement, you need to use a plastic candlecup; these are readily available from florists and can also be used to convert other containers such as wine bottles and narrow-necked vases into candleholders. They are small, round dishes with a cork-shaped 'plug' that fits into the candlestick or other container, and an indentation to hold a cylinder of florist's foam.

When the piece of foam you use to support both the flower stems and the candles is very narrow there can be problems with its splitting and breaking up, even if you pare the base of the candle to reduce its girth. One way to avoid this happening is to use a plastic candle spike, also available from florists. Usually in bright, or dark green, these spikes are tapered to a very narrow point and have a small cylindrical holder that just fits a standard candle.

CONCEALED CANDLEHOLDERS
If the flowers hide the candleholder, it doesn't matter what sort you use, as long as the candleholder is stable and concealed completely.

You can also improvise a base by combining a candleholder and outer container, such as the shallow china dish featured, or even a glass ashtray. Make sure that the candleholder is held firmly in place, especially if the display has to be moved once it has been made. Affix the candleholder to the base with strips of florist's adhesive tape, or wedge it in place with florist's foam blocks, as shown in the steps on page 175.

CANDLE WAX WATCHPOINT
You can buy non-drip candles, but if you get wax drips on your tablecloth, lift off the surface deposit with your fingernails. Place clean blotting paper over and under the area, and iron it, with the temperature set on low. Keep moving the paper as the melted wax is absorbed; remove the final traces with grease solvent and wash or dry clean as normal. Test the grease solvent first on a small corner of the fabric to make sure the solvent will not harm the material.

In this way you can utilise a wide variety of decorative and household articles as candle bases and bring a touch of individuality to your designs.

CHOOSING THE CANDLES
White candles are always elegant but coloured candles can be effective if co-ordinated with the flowers. Try to avoid clashing colours; pink candles, for example can differ considerably. If using a particular shade of candles, take them with you when you pick out the flowers.

Heavily decorated candles may detract from the flowers, especially if combined with ornate candlesticks. Try to keep candles and holders simple.

Whatever candles you choose, make sure they are vertical. Line the candles up with a door or window frame and, if using more than one candle, line them up with each other. Unless the display is front facing, walk around it to check the candles from every direction.

It might be possible to match the candles exactly to one of the flower colours – a purple anemone, for example – or even to a secondary colour in the flowers, such as the brilliant yellow centres of white spray chrysanthemums, or the vibrant scarlet streaks in two-tone carnations or pinks.

It can also be effective to choose candles in more than one colour, teaming them with flowers in a single shade. If, for example, you are composing a group of candlesticks arranged with all-blue anemones, you could evoke the many colours normally associated with these flowers, and use a mauve candle, a purple one, and so on. Again, if you are arranging all-white flowers on a table set with a wonderful cloth or patterned china, you could echo these colours in your choice of candles and achieve a pleasingly harmonious and unusual effect.

CHOOSING THE FLOWERS AND FOLIAGE

In the second display, roses, anemones and bouvardia are used with leather leaf fern and bear grass. Candleholder displays can be just as attractive with just one type of flower and foliage, as shown in the other two arrangements.

Roses and fern are available all year round. As anemones are seasonal, use florist's Turk's cap ranunculus, globe flowers, Japanese anemones or single garden roses instead. Bouvardia usually has to be ordered; suitable substitutes include larkspur, verbena and phlox. In place of the bear grass, try delicate blades of Japanese sweet flag (*Acorus gramineus* 'Variegatus').

Whatever combination of flowers and foliage you choose, try to achieve a pleasing contrast of colour, shape and texture. In our display on the right, the minute-flowered bouvardia shows like tiny stars against the stark contrast of the glossy leaves; the flat-faced anemones and full, round roses perfectly complement the bouvardia clusters in the second display, and each rose is seen to full advantage against the mixed foliage in the china dish design.

CHOOSING THE SETTING

The dining-room table is the traditional setting for flowers and candles, but they could be placed on a sideboard or buffet table. A mantelpiece is a good position for a long, narrow arrangement. If you intend to light the candles, consider the safety factor. Positioning lit candles on a low coffee table, for example, would make them vulnerable to accidental knocks, especially if young children are around.

Consider placing a candle arrangement on a wide windowsill, or placing stubby candles on either side of a taller flower display in the window. It is an idea that is popular in Scandinavian countries, and one which signals a cheerful welcome to guests and gives pleasure to passers-by. A note of caution: keep lighted candles well away from curtain material.

MAKING TWO BEAUTIFUL CANDLE AND FLOWER DISPLAYS

1 Place a small glass candleholder in the centre of a shallow white dish and hold it securely in place with strips of florist's adhesive tape. Put two small blocks of florist's foam on either side of the candleholder and secure with more adhesive tape. Select a tall white candle and trim the end so that it fits firmly into the candleholder.

2 Begin disguising both blocks of florist's foam with leather leaf foliage. Place ten stems, about 8cm (3 in) in length, around the edge of the foam to form a collar, overlapping the container's edge. Cut some shorter stems of the leather leaf fern to about 2.5cm (1 in) in length. Insert these so they radiate out from the centre towards the sides, covering the florist's foam.

3 Cut the stems of 11 pink rose buds to a length of 12cm (5 in). Place two roses on either side of the candle. Arrange the rest on the centre of the dish and around the edges so that the heads of the roses face outwards and soften the white rim of the container. Try to keep the flowers and foliage low around the base of the candle so it can burn for as long as possible.

LEFT A single, tall white candle forms the central focus of attention and dominates this horizontal arrangement of roses and leather leaf fern.

1 Cut florist's foam to fit snugly into the centre of a four-stick candleholder. Secure in position with florist's adhesive tape. Trim sprigs of leather leaf fern to 8cm (3 in) and insert into the edges of the foam to form a collar, using shorter leaves for the central area. Trim eight bear grass stems to a length of 12cm (5 in) and arrange them to fan out from the centre.

2 Cut five pink roses to 12cm (5 in); position one in the centre of the foam and surround it with four more. Cut three stems of bouvardia to the same height and arrange near the centre of the display. Remove most of the foliage from four more stems of bouvardia, trim down to 5cm (2 in) and arrange around the base of the display.

3 Lastly, add about six anemones in a range of pink shades. Arrange the flowers on two levels throughout the display. The stems should range from 10cm (4 in) to 8cm (3 in). Inspect the display to ensure all the gaps are filled. Don't allow the candles to burn down too low or the flames will singe the flowers.

ABOVE Four candles, in a glass ring candleholder, emerge from a generous array of roses, anemones and bouvardia, with a central 'foundation' of bear grass and collar of leather leaf fern.

Table Settings

The rules which govern dinner-table arrangements are dictated by common sense. A tall arrangement like the candelabrum opposite, is fine so long as the guests are spaced sufficiently far apart to be able to converse around it.

Low, flat arrangements are easy to see over but should not extend so far that leafy tendrils trail in the food. Chunky arrangements should not be so large that they leave insufficient space on the table.

A lovely option, especially for weddings and other special occasions, is the formal, lollipop-style display: a tall, slender, central stem topped by a florist's-foam sphere covered in fresh or dried flowers, with ribbons trailing down from a bow tied just under the sphere. The guests can then see each other's faces and there's more room for food than with a conventional centre-piece, and as an additional advantage, the feeling of festivity is enhanced.

Before thinking about the flowers, it is vital to consider the table itself: how large it is, how many people are dining, where the place settings will fall, whether food will be served from a sideboard or put on the table, how much passing of dishes the meal will involve, and so on. In this way it is possible to see exactly how much space, and what shape of space, is available for flowers, and then to decide on the flowers and containers.

ABOVE LEFT Spectacular white flowers interspersed with slim white tapers surround a hurricane lantern to create a fabulous al-fresco display.
LEFT A pretty wicker basket is the ideal receptacle for an array of flowers, perfect for a lunch-time party.
RIGHT Sweetly fragrant and timelessly popular sweet peas gracefully adorn a silver candelabrum for a formal dinner-table.

Festive Focal Point

WHILE YOUR DINNER GUESTS ARE WAITING FOR THE FIRST COURSE, LET THEM ENJOY THIS
BEAUTIFUL ARRANGEMENT OF FRESH SEASONAL FRUIT AND FLOWERS

Fruit and flowers are a very traditional decorative display combination, as beautiful today as they were a hundred years ago, when the Victorians made fruit and flower displays on tiered ornamental stands, or epergnes. Their display ideas for parties were truly original and here is a modern interpretation of the theme that makes a tempting table centrepiece for a dinner party.

The display is all-round and informal, built on two florist's foam blocks, taped to a flat, round serving tray. Four small wicker baskets are wired around the edge of the blocks. A generous, round mass of fresh flowers and foliage is built up around the baskets, concealing the foundation and, finally, the baskets are filled with fruit.

You can make the basic display on the morning of the party, or even the night before, if you've got somewhere cool to keep it, but you should wait until the last minute to add the fruit as cut fruit discolours very quickly and would ruin the spectacular look of the display.

CHOOSING THE FLOWERS
A cool green, yellow and white scheme is appropriate for late summer evenings, but you could substitute pink or blue for the yellow, or eliminate the third colour, and stick to white and green.

White bridal gladioli have a delicacy lacking in large-flowered forms. Spiky flowers with a similar form include montbretia, schizostylis and ixia (African corn lily). For a cheaper alternative, use white spray carnations.

Short-stemmed, creamy white and yellow hybrid roses add a touch of romance. Pure white or pink roses could be used. Another alternative is to buy spray roses, with several small blossoms per stem; they're more expensive, but you need fewer stems. For a cheaper ingredient, use godetias or scented pinks.

ADDED FRAGRANCE
Yellow freesias add fragrance and beauty; white, cream or mauve freesias could be used or multi-coloured bunches. For a long-lasting alternative, use green-white chincherinchees.

Singapore orchids are amazingly cheap in this country, considering their exotic origins and appearance. As well as the white featured here, they come in yellow, acid green, shades of purple and a peach colour. Florists sell them in single-colour and mixed bunches.

White lilies add contrasting scale, but yellow or pink ones could be substituted. For additional fragrance, choose 'Stargazer' lilies; however, use them sparingly as they are quite expensive.

Moluccella, or bells of Ireland, seems an unlikely ingredient, since it's enormously tall compared to the other flowers. Here, it's cut into three pieces, and used to infill the arrangement. A suitable alternative would be to use stems of round-leaved eucalyptus.

Blue-dyed gypsophila is the most unusual flower in the arrangement and is used for its light airy appeal. White gypsophila or fennel flowers also would provide a lacy touch.

CHOOSING THE FOLIAGE
Bear grass, like the moluccella, is too long to be used its natural length in the design, so it is cut into thirds and inserted to make a pretty, linear fountain over the flowers. Slender stems of broom or ornamental grass, such as variegated sedge or pampas grass, could be substituted.

Ivy from the garden, or from a house plant in need of pruning, is used as filler foliage, and to soften the outline of the display. Variegated ivy or the pretty yellow cultivar 'Buttercup' could be subistituted.

WIRING FRESH FRUIT

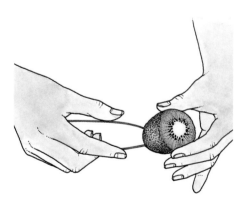

As well as displaying small fruits alongside the flowers in open baskets, make them an integral part of the arrangement. Wire fruits, such as gooseberries, lychees, strawberries, kumquats and grapes, on lengths of stub wire and insert the wire stems into the foam. The bright colours and varied textures of the fruit skins will contrast with the softer colours of the flowers.

For a stunning, but short-lived effect, cut fruits, such as kiwi fruit, in half to reveal the attractive inner flesh. Wire each half separately on lengths of stub wire. Push the wire through the base of the fruit and bend into a hairpin shape. Replace frequently as the fruit's flesh will discolour quickly.

MAKING A FLOWER AND FRUIT FOCAL POINT

1 Soak two blocks of florist's foam. Tape them, side by side to a small serving tray. Holding the tray firmly, attach a heart-shaped basket to the foam at the front using two stub wires inserted into the foam through the base of the basket. Secure the two cornucopia-style baskets at either side and one round basket to the back, attached in the same way.

4 Cut four white roses and insert them vertically above the heart-shaped basket. Cut another four stems short and place three in a cluster to one side of the basket and one single rose on the other side. Cut the bridal gladioli to even lengths and frame the central basket with the flowers inserted in a soft fan shape.

INGREDIENTS

1 *4 bunches of bridal gladioli*
2 *12 white roses*
3 *5 bunches of freesias*
4 *3 stems of Singapore orchids*
5 *1 bunch of white lilies*
6 *1 yellow rose*
7 *4 stems of* Cineraria maritima
8 *¼ bunch of blue-dyed gypsophila*
9 *1 stem of moluccella*
10 *5 stems of bear grass*
11 *3 stems of asparagus fern*
12 *6 trails of ivy*
13 *a small bunch of grapes*
14 *4 passion fruits*
15 *a handful of cherries*
16 *a punnet of raspberries*
17 *4 small assorted wicker baskets*
18 *stub wires*
19 *tray*
20 *2 blocks of florist's foam*
21 *scissors*
22 *florist's adhesive tape*

2 Snip trails of ivy from an ivy house plant and insert all over the foam to trail over the edge of the tray. Frame the central heart-shaped basket with short stems of *Cineraria maritima* foliage. Cut a moluccella stem into three pieces and place behind the basket, one piece hanging over the display side.

3 Snip a stem of asparagus fern into small pieces. Dot it around the display. Cut the stems of bear grass into equal lengths. Insert them into the middle of the foam so that they spray out fountain-like over the other foliage material, adding a contrast in height to lift the design. Spray the foliage as you work to keep it fresh.

CHOOSING THE FRUIT

Grapes, passion fruit, cherries and raspberries are shown in the tempting nibble baskets, but a wide range of exotic and seasonal fruits are available from large supermarkets and street markets.

Grapes are available all year round; in cool green or rich, warm red. Cut them into small clusters, so that they are distributed evenly throughout the design and so that they are not all eaten at once. You could fill each basket with a different variety of grape, perhaps including a few grape leaves and curly tendrils from an ornamental vine in the display. Black cherries are shown, but you could use scarlet or red-flushed white Kent cherries.

Raspberries are delightful, but blackberries or any one of numerous hybrid berries are available – tayberries, dewberries, loganberries or sunberries – all can be used instead.

For a more integrated look in your display, you could wire up small individual fruits in complementary or contrasting colours – see box – and insert them among the flowers.

ALTERNATIVE NIBBLES

For an autumnal display or Christmas table, fill the basket with a selection of nuts, such as walnuts, hazel nuts, pistachios, Brazil or pecan nuts, in shades of beige and brown, and change the colour scheme of the flowers accordingly – rust-coloured chrysanthemums would be ideal.

At any time of year, you could fill the baskets with a selection of appetizers such as crisps, peanuts, Japanese rice crackers or Bombay mix. For a truly luxurious touch, fill each basket with cooked and chilled giant Pacific prawns, garnished with lemon wedges. Alternatively, fill the baskets with wrapped mints, chocolates or sugared almonds, to accompany after-dinner coffee and drinks.

5 Insert one yellow rose to the right-hand side of the basket. Cut the freesia stems at a slant and insert throughout the arrangement. The freesias' soft stems may need to be wired as they tend to snap. Yellow freesias are the best choice as they are much more fragrant than the other varieties.

6 Cut the stems of blue-dyed gypsophila into small sprigs and insert throughout the display. This provides light touches of blue to contrast with the yellow and cream colour scheme. Cut each Singapore orchid spray in two. Place one half on either side of the display. Fill each basket with tempting small fruits.

CHOOSING THE CONTAINER

The arrangement shown features circular, heart-shaped and cornucopia wicker baskets but four identical baskets would work just as well. It's easy to wire wicker baskets in place, and, unlike plastic containers, they look as attractive empty as full.

Celebratory Arrangement

CAPTURE THE JOY OF A CELEBRATION WITH THIS FORMAL DISPLAY OF FRESH FLOWERS, SET IN AN
ELEGANT SILVER PUNCH BOWL

Beautifully-arranged flowers can make any celebration especially memorable, and you can continue to enjoy the arrangement after the event. The arrangement here is designed specifically for a christening, but could equally well be used for a formal dinner-party.

Flower arrangements for spring celebrations are particularly easy to create; florist's shops are full of small, delicate flowers. White, pastel blue and pink are the traditional choices for a christening and these hues also suit a subtle but stylish dinner-party display. In the featured display, yellow and white flowers are used.

CHOOSING THE FLOWERS
You could use blue or yellow flowers, alone or with white, or an all-white arrangement, since white floral arrangements can look extremely stunning. Pale peach or peach and white displays are also attractive or use a multi-coloured scheme, with pale pink, peach, yellow, mauve, blue and white flowers.

THE MAIN INGREDIENT
Cream spray carnations form the backbone of this display. Buy two bunches, with some flowers half open, and others in bud. Spray carnations come in many shades so you could use lemon, pale pink, peach or pure white ones. For a less formal display, use single, white, daisy-like spray chrysanthemums. When you get the spray carnations home, snip the ends off the stems part-way between the fat nodes, and give them a long drink of water.

Two bunches of creamy-lemon 'Fantasy' freesias are included for their sweet fragrance and their large double blooms. Buy freesias when the lowest flowers are open, and the next few buds are showing colour. Less spectacular, single freesias could be used instead but avoid mixed bunches with predominantly dark red and purple blooms, as these will over-power the other flowers subtle tones. When you get freesias home, snip off the stem ends and give them a long drink of water.

DELICATE TOUCH
Gypsophila is ideal for filling out an arrangement because of its delicate airy appearance. Buy four, large, well-branched stems, with the flowers half to two-thirds open. There are single and double-flowered varieties in pink, creamy-white and pure white as well as dyed types in blue, violet or bright red.

A dozen white roses and 20 miniature yellow roses are required. These are the most expensive ingredients, but worth it for a truly special occasion. The roses used here are shown at a more mature stage, to indicate the finished effect, but for the longest display time, buy roses in tight bud, before the petals start to separate. When you get them home, re-cut the ends, remove the lower leaves, and give them a long drink of water.

Asparagus fern adds a touch of lacy greenery, in keeping with the delicate flowers. You need ten stems for this display, and may have to order them in advance. There are several suitable forms of asparagus fern.

Finally, add long, training cream ribbons attached to wire stems that can cascade over the rim of the best silver bowl you can beg, borrow or steal, to provide a festive touch to this celebratory display.

MAKING RIBBON BOWS

1 Hold the length of ribbon between your forefinger and thumb, leaving the ends long enough to trail, form two loops. Cut the ribbon ends to leave two 13-17cm (5-7in) ends to trail to the base of the display.

2 Bend the stub wire in half, and place it behind the ribbon where the loops meet. Secure the loops by wrapping one end of the wire around the base. Twist the wires to form a 'stem' to insert into the display.

CREATING A CELEBRATORY PARTY-TABLE ARRANGEMENT

1 Thoroughly soak one and a half blocks of florist's foam. Cut the smaller block in half. Push each block firmly into the mixing bowl, the large block in the middle flanked by the two smaller pieces. Secure them firmly with two 25cm (10in) strips of florist's tape. Carefully place the mixing bowl inside the silver punch bowl.

4 The pale freesias complement the carnations. Trim the freesia stems to different lengths and insert them alongside the carnations. Insert them at various angles to build up the round symmetrical shape. Have a wide sweep of freesias above the lowest circle of carnations to form the full, creamy base of the display.

INGREDIENTS

1 10 asparagus fern stems
2 10 creamy-yellow 'Fantasy' freesias
3 4 sprays of gypsophila
4 8 stems of spray carnations
5 12 white roses
6 20 yellow miniature roses
7 silver punch bowl
8 glass mixing bowl
9 1m (3 ft) of cream ribbon
10 florist's foam
11 florist's adhesive
12 scissors
13 stub wires

2 Trim eight stems of asparagus fern to 20cm (8 in). Position them around the edge of the foam, encouraging them to hang over the edge. This creates a soft collar to hide the rim of the bowl and forms a feathery outline. Cut the shoots off the remaining stems and insert them into the foam, making a leafy base to conceal the foam and the bowl.

3 Cut eight stems of spray carnations to various lengths between 15-25cm (6-10 in). Arch the longer stems downwards over the edge around the outside of the display and position the shorter stems at various angles towards the centre. Use these less expensive spray flowers to set the arrangement's height and establish the shape.

CHOOSING THE CONTAINER

A simple, round container suits the round build-up of flowers. A raised, silver, punch bowl is shown here, but an alabaster or pewter bowl would be equally effective. If you are having caterers to do your food, ask them about hiring a silver punch bowl, or, alternatively hire one from an independent firm, or borrow one from friends or relatives. As an alternative, you can use an old-fashioned round soup tureen with a small inbuilt pedestal or a flat-based plain china or delicately-patterned porcelain bowl. Avoid anything boldly-coloured or rustic, such as stoneware.

If you use a silver bowl, you will also need an inner, waterproof bowl to prevent the silver from tarnishing. A glass mixing bowl is shown, but any bowl that fitted comfortably inside the outer container would be suitable. Place a small pad of soft cloth between the two bowls, to prevent the inner bowl slipping or scratching the outer one.

CHOOSING THE SETTING

The arrangement makes an ideal, front-facing centrepiece for a buffet table, drinks table or sideboard. It is also a perfect all-round display for a free-standing table, such as a table in the middle of a dining room.

IN PERFECT HARMONY

It is a good idea to create harmonizing flower displays for both the celebratory table and the rest of your home if you are having a really formal dinner-party.

If you or one of your family or friends are arranging a pedestal arrangement as well as the rounded one, you can take a cue from this display and create a design in a similar vein. Outline the dome shape with sprays of dainty fern – nothing too solid or heavy, in view of the occasion – and fill in the shape with, say, carnations, roses and spray chrysanthemums. In spring you could include delicate paper-white and pale cream narcissi, which have a lovely subtle scent.

If you like you could compose a complementary floral ring to hang on a wall, arranging the flower stems in blocks of foam.

5 Brighten the display with the gold miniature roses. Trim their stems, insert some around the outside and fill in the central shape by nestling the rest among the foliage, freesias and carnations. The vivid colour emphasizes the yellow centres of the freesias. Trim the stems of the white roses and place them throughout the display to add lustre.

6 Cut the gypsophila sprays into many small offshoots. Trim them to 15cm-25cm (6-10in) and scatter them through the other flowers, creating a soft haze over the display. To break up the harsh surface of the bowl and finish the display, place the ribbon bows (see box) at even intervals around the outside of the bowl, letting the long ribbon ends trail.

Index